ROADMAP

The **GET-IT-TOGETHER GUIDE** for **FIGURING OUT WHAT TO DO** with **YOUR LIFE**

by **ROADTRIP NATION**

Created by Nathan Gebhard, Brian McAllister, and Mike Marriner

with

Jay Sacher, Alyssa Frank, Annie Mais, Jamie Zehler, and Willie Witte

CHRONICLE BOOKS

SAN FRANCISCO

Library of Congress Cataloging-in-Publication Data:
McAllister, Brian, 1975-
Roadmap : the get-it-together guide for figuring out what to do with your life / by Roadtrip Nation ; created by Brian McAllister, Mike Marriner, and Nathan Gebhard with Jay Sacher, Alyssa Frank, Annie Mais, Jamie Zehler, and Willie Witte.
pages cm
ISBN 978-1-4521-2845-0
Includes bibliographical references and index.
1. Career development. 2. Vocational guidance. I. Roadtrip Nation (Organization) II. Title.
HF5381.M39623 2015
650.1—dc23   2015006850

Manufactured in China

Designed by Jennifer Tolo Pierce
Illustrations by Matthew Allen

Interviewees' quotes from the Roadtrip Nation Interview Archive appear throughout this book and have been edited for print purposes. Videos of the interviews can be viewed at **www.roadtripnation.com/explore**.

10 9 8 7 6 5 4

Chronicle Books LLC
680 Second Street
San Francisco, California 94107
www.chroniclebooks.com

WE WROTE THIS BOOK FOR YOU, SO MAKE IT YOURS.

Scrawl notes in the margins, dog-ear chapters, stain pages with coffee, throw it against the wall if you feel like it. You're steering the wheel, so take charge.

Above all, be honest. Everything you do in these pages will be about silencing the din you hear from others and turning what makes you unique—the interests, values, motivations, and peculiar quirks only you know and understand—into a life you want to live. It's an investigatory journey that'll lead you to a path that's most true to who you are, but it's bound to stir up some deep questions in the process. Don't ignore those questions. Examine them. Build on them. And let us know what you find.

See you on the Open Road.

—Roadtrip Nation

#RoadmapBook

@RoadtripNation

facebook.com/roadtripnation

instagram.com/roadtripnation

contents

PART THREE: BECOME

PROJECTS

ABOUT ROADTRIP NATION

Roadtrip Nation started in 2001 when a group of lost and confused friends took a Roadtrip to figure out what to do with their lives. The idea was simple: talk to people who do what they love and get a better understanding of how to create a life you want to lead. We came to call the people we interviewed Roadtrip Nation Leaders. They were from all walks of life but had one thing in common: They were leaders in a new way of living. They built lives centered on their interests and propelled by their individuality. They were doctors, writers, corporate moguls, monks, musicians, engineers, judges, astrobiologists, hairstylists, lawyers, filmmakers, athletes, entrepreneurs, and others who shared stories of the paths they took, the mistakes they made, and the myths they debunked.

road trip
noun
A journey made by car, bus, etc.

Roadtrip
noun
The experience of defining your own life.

An experience of travel (short or long distances) to interview individuals who live meaningful lives getting paid to do what they love.

What began as one Roadtrip turned into a movement, including an annual documentary series on public television, a number of books (including this one), online resources for self-discovery, and a growing Interview Archive of stories from the road—all dedicated to helping individuals define their own roads in life.

In 2009, the movement expanded into education with the creation of The Roadtrip Nation Experience, a self-discovery program for the classroom designed to help students explore their identities and find pathways aligned with their interests by conducting interviews with Leaders in their own communities.

Today, Roadtrip Nation continues to empower individuals to create meaningful lives doing what they love.

To learn more about the movement, visit **www.roadtripnation.com**.

For more information about Roadtrip Nation in education, visit **www.roadtripnation.org**

THE ROADTRIP NATION
INTERVIEW ARCHIVE

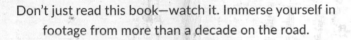

Don't just read this book—watch it. Immerse yourself in footage from more than a decade on the road.

With the purchase of this book you get a free limited membership to the Roadtrip Nation Interview Archive. There you can watch thousands of videos featuring people who have built livelihoods around their interests, including all of the interviews referenced in this book and more than a hundred episodes from our television series.

To get started, explore videos by Interest, Foundation, and Theme.

Have this book with you and log onto **www.roadtripnation.com /roadmapbook**. Use the following code and you'll be ready to go.

[**WYR-SC9-CE3-978**]

INTRODUCTION

This book is about answering an old question in a new way.

The question itself is unavoidable; no matter who you are or where you're from or what you've been through, you're going to reach a moment in life when you're anxious and confused, unsure about the path ahead. And you're going to hear that voice, from outside and within, asking you, "So, what are you going to do with your life?"

It's not easy to admit that often the only honest answer to that question is "I don't know." It's tough being lost. We speak from experience—and we're not just referring to heading down the wrong street or being in the wrong city, or even state (although we've been there plenty of times). We're talking about that deeper meaning of lost, the one that prompts the scary questions about life and work and lasting satisfaction.

We've been lost, and we've asked ourselves and others those difficult questions for years. When you're facing the future, when those questions are barreling down on you and the knots in your stomach are tightening, you can feel incredibly isolated. We're here to remind you that you're not alone.

At Roadtrip Nation, we've spent more than a decade tasking ourselves—and a growing movement of young Roadtrippers—to explore how others have learned to live fulfilling lives. Through their stories, we've learned that it's absolutely possible to live a rich and considered life—one that will grow and thrive along with your interests, your values, and your vision. We know it because we've sat face-to-face with people who are doing just that, and we've straight-up asked them what it takes to live a life that's both meaningful and an expression of one's individuality.

Do you have any regrets?

HOW DID YOU BUILD A LIFE AROUND YOUR INTERESTS AND YOUR INDIVIDUALITY?

HOW DID YOU DEAL WITH OTHER PEOPLE'S EXPECTATIONS OF YOU?

The people we met and continue to meet are living with intention—not just balancing work and life, but integrating them in a way that is true, unique, and sustainable. These Roadtrip Nation Leaders provided us with new answers to old questions. And frankly, those new answers arrived just in time.

The world has changed. The old, secure model for building a life that past generations had access to is long gone. Once upon a time, you could train for a job, get that job, and stay put for the rest of your life, ambling off to the shuffleboards of retirement with a pension in hand at the end of the ride. That *Leave It to Beaver* suburban fairy tale went belly-up with the rotary phone.

Generations since then have received a lot of lip service about new ways of entering the "workforce" and building "careers," but really, most of what we get is the same old picket-fence template left over from another time. Today, just as they did thirty years ago, high school kids fill in arbitrary bubbles on personality tests that tell them what occupation they're "best suited" for, despite the fact that those bubbles and the accompanying results rarely speak to any deep truth about their identities. They are expected to move through accepted motions and slot themselves into preprogrammed lifestyles with the assumption that going from A to B will lead them to C.

HOW DID YOU KNOW WHEN TO MAKE A CHANGE?

WHEN HAVE YOU FAILED?

What exactly is success to you?

HOW DID YOU BLOCK OUT THE NOISE OF OTHERS and LISTEN TO YOURSELF?

WHAT WOULD YOU HAVE DONE DIFFERENTLY?

A ⟶ B ⟶

C

Wherever following point A to point B is supposed to take you, the destination you hope for won't be the same by the time you've finished reading this book. Things are changing fast. While even the most thickheaded of us can see that the old model is broken, nothing substantial has emerged to replace it, except a vague sense of unease and a lot of nervous societal hand-wringing. To make matters worse, our marketing-driven culture beats images of "success" into our brains every day. The ideal becomes consumption: Get the SUV with the shiny rims or the newest smartphone, stay up on the latest trends, go for the instant fix. Thanks to technology, these trends are coming at us from every angle and at an exponentially growing rate. This is a dangerous and damaging combination of influences, and if you're finding yourself overwhelmed by it, that's okay. So were we. It's exactly why we took the first Roadtrip. And it's why we wrote this book.

Back at the beginning (just as now) we craved the breathing room, the thinking space, and the fresh perspectives that the Open Road had to offer. We felt that there must be more options than what we'd been exposed to, more examples of people out there we could learn from. Adrift, without a steady paycheck or a backup plan, we jumped into an RV with nothing but a nagging sense that how we'd been taught to think about our futures was in fact deeply wrong. So we hit the road to find the people who'd made it to the other side, somehow— the people who were actually living lives that were deeply satisfying. People like the chairman of Starbucks, the creator of Spawn, National Geographic photographers, an editorial cartoonist, a race-car mechanic, Madonna's stylist, the scientist who decoded the human genome, TV personalities, a lobsterman on the coast of Maine, a director of *Saturday Night Live*, public radio hosts, and the guy who directed the landing of the Mars *Curiosity* rover.

We asked them questions. Lots of questions. Where were you at our age? How did you get to where you are today? Were you ever scared or unsure? Did you ever feel like you were pressured to conform? How do you deal with the uncertainty and ambiguity of life? What exactly is "success" to you? Are you happy? When have you failed? What do you wish you knew when you were our age? How did you turn your beliefs into action?

Their responses to those questions became the foundation that Roadtrip Nation has been built on, and as you turn the pages of this book, you'll hear more and more of the insights and stories that have been shared with us on the road.

The original Roadtrip acted as a launchpad for the movement that Roadtrip Nation has become.

Now, more than a decade later, a small army of soul-searching Roadtrippers have been behind the wheels of our Green RVs. Together we've crisscrossed this massive country (and a couple of other continents) and amassed an extensive archive of interviews compiling tons of voices that have inspired and engaged us over the years.

What we've learned—what we are still learning—is at the heart of this book. It's all centered around something we've come to call **Self-Construction**. What we started to see was that there was in fact a process to living a sustainable, fulfilling life, one that strives to build not "work-life balance" but what we call a meaningful Worklife. The kind of Worklife that ensures when the alarm rings in the morning you don't feel dread at starting another day, but rather excitement about the path you're on.

In its most basic form, this process involves **letting go** of any misaligned ideas about yourself, **defining** who you are at your core, and then **becoming** the next version of yourself (plus starting over when things get off track). It wasn't exactly a linear, easy-to-codify progression that was ripe for automatic implementation, but it was there. Common threads began to emerge, as did common actions, ideas, and questions. We started to get *really* excited. These weren't just stories we were compiling, but concrete examples of how to live.

What emerged was a circular, endlessly renewable approach that you can use to stay on the path toward a meaningful and inspired life. And that's the key: Self-Construction starts with you. Everything begins with your personal interests and values and builds out from there. Despite what others try to tell you, there is no blueprint that works for everyone. It's an interactive, ever-evolving process that only you can start and only you can finish. You'll have to ask yourself some difficult questions and confront the answers you get, no matter how challenging they may be. After all, you are the only constant in your life. You must build your own authentic experiences rather than live those others wish you to. It's not your parents' life, not society's, not what the media tries to tell you your life should be, not even what we say it should be.

Self-Construction is about focusing on the core of your individuality and what matters to you. With hard work, and plenty of course correction, this focus will lead to the most meaningful experiences, the most enriching work, and the most fulfilling life you can have.

Despite some people's impression of us, we're actually quite realistic people (we can even be cynical at times). We understand that no matter what your circumstances are, forging a life path that's right for you can seem impossible. Most people, ourselves included, find big, high roadblocks between where they are and where they want to be. Responsibilities, expectations, self-doubt, and the grind of everyday life can make us feel trapped and confused. We get worn down and worn out, and we feel tempted to give up. We start to believe that maybe there is no realistic way (beyond dumb luck) to live a life that's both fulfilling and financially sustainable.

One foggy morning, when road-tripping through the redwoods of Northern California, we expressed these exact feelings to a man named John Perry Barlow.* This free-thinking, philosophizing Renaissance man has traveled many differ-ent roads in life. From early beginnings as a cattle rancher and lyricist for the Grateful Dead, to pioneering internet activism and cofounding the Electronic Frontier Foundation, John's rambling life story had our heads spinning. We came to him panicked and paralyzed by the confusion ahead of us, and like a modern-day mountaintop guru, his thoughts gave us peace and clarity: "I think

 www.roadtripnation.com/leader/john-perry-barlow

the most important thing is to recognize that everybody else is scared, too. It's not like you're the only ones who feel like they don't get it. Nobody really gets it. It's not gettable. **All you can really do is try to make a warm peace with all the rest of your confused and frightened peers, and take courage and comfort in that."**

Much of this book is about courageously taking comfort in our collective confusion and refuge in the guidance and wisdom of those who have gone before us. John told us, "I think it's important to place a different value on what you connote when you say 'getting lost.' As long as we assume that that means we are helpless, and adrift, and abandoned, then very little good can come of it. But start to think about being lost in a positive way—[it's about] exploring and opening yourself up to possibilities that you wouldn't have otherwise considered. **If you're not lost, you're not much of an explorer."**

We value exploration, and thus we value getting lost. Since you're reading this, there's a good chance you do, too. Because the flip side of the new world landscape before us today is an immense space for creativity and flexibility, and endless possibility for experimentation and exploration. The world is changing rapidly, and it is ripe for us to shape it to our liking. Upcoming generations can, and should, create livelihoods that have never been seen before. And that is pretty damn exciting.

Immersed in the stories we've heard, we feel compelled to share them, but we also feel a powerful sense of responsibility to find our own ways. It's impossible to listen to the people we've met and not be provoked to act, to move, to become something more than we were yesterday. That's the energy and enthusiasm we want to share with you.

Self-Construction never stops. There's no finish line. Life is an open-ended pursuit that constantly leads us to new truths, and those truths can only come from within ourselves. This book is simply meant to be used as a guide to your own Self-Construction. Interact with it. Question it. Question us. Use it as you see fit. Use it, then step back and reevaluate your life. Then reuse it. Then step back and reevaluate your life. Then reuse it. Then step back and reevaluate your life. Then reuse it. Then reuse it. Then reuse it. Then reuse it. . . . You get the idea.

Repeatedly revisiting the ideas on these pages will challenge the way you see the world. Let these concepts help you continually build a life that is wholly yours.

Come get lost with us. You may be surprised where you find yourself.

LET

PART ONE :::::::::::::::::::::::::::

CHAPTER 1

THE INVISIBLE ASSEMBLY LINE

Here's a big, goofy cliché: *you can be whomever you want to be.* We just cringed as we wrote that, but nevertheless it happens to be true.

So how did this corny afterschool-special cliché become a tired trope rather than an empowering truism? Maybe because the world we navigate forces us to ignore its underlying truth. In the name of security, we put aside what we might truly want. We pay our dues. We put our heads down and work hard, chugging along on a preplotted path that promises stability, security, and comfort. But in the quiet moments, we have a nagging feeling. Is this the path we're supposed to be on? Are we fulfilled? Satisfied? Are we living our lives or are our lives living us? Are there choices we could be making that better speak to who we are? Are we on the right road?

For some people, finding the "right" road is easy (or at least it seems like it to those of us standing off on the side). They seem to be living the life they want to live, they appear to be successful, thriving, and happy in the roles they've chosen. For most of us, however, finding that road feels like an exercise in impossibility. We get stuck. And lost. We feel afraid of the unknown or incapable of bold action. We become bogged down by the responsibilities we face and the choices in front of us.

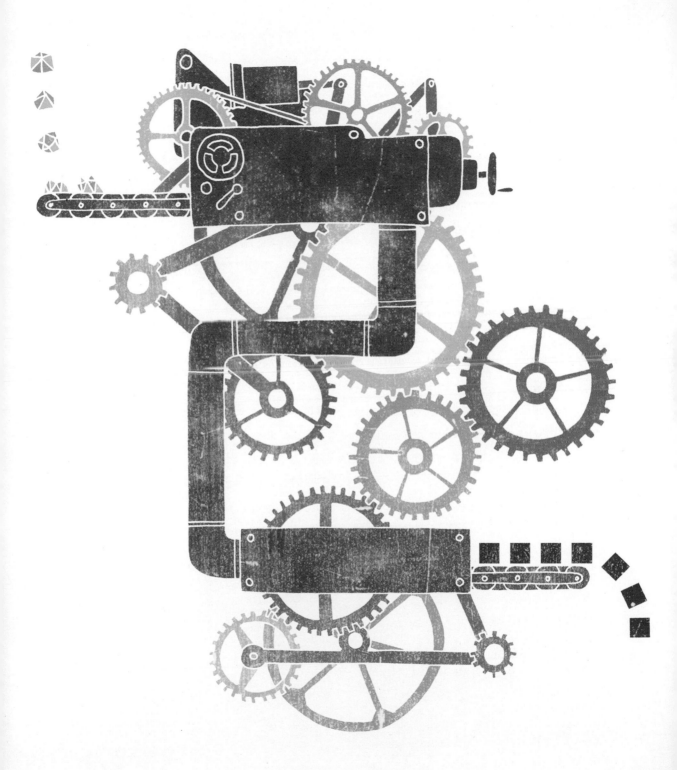

If the road belongs to us, why is it so difficult to get on it? Why can't we force that cliché back into truth? The answer lies in a particularly sneaky aspect of human nature. Just as a deluge of rain pounding a dry hillside will form into rivulets that trickle downhill—beating tracks of least resistance into the earth—as individuals, we tend to fall into the paths that society has already created for us. This process starts early in our lives and is devilishly hard to shake. And while there can be value in the tried-and-true (there's nothing wrong with everybody wearing pants, for instance), following by rote restricts individual experience and inhibits potential.

Think about it this way: If you live on the North American continent, outside your door is a road that will get you to New York City. You can pull out a map and take any route you want, winding through purple mountain majesties and amber waves of whatnot and stopping at as many roadside tourist traps as you'd like. You can explore sleepy towns off the beaten path, you can stop off for a few cheesesteaks in Philly or roll up to the Grand Tetons, and no matter where you happen to be, you will still be on the road to New York City. But if you punch your destination into your phone's GPS, it will lead you directly to the closest highway. It will tell you exactly how far it is to New York and estimate exactly how long it will take you to get there. And it will be a nonstop march that's as straight as possible. You'll have certainty but no cheesesteaks, no time for exploring, just you in your car on the very same highway that everybody

else takes. This is exactly what society's formula for "success" is like: a one-size-fits-all, bumper-to-bumper haul that ignores the nuances of who you really are.

This is the Invisible Assembly Line, and chances are you're on it.

Our personal Assembly Lines are built cog by cog from all the expectations, education, societal gimmicks, well-meaning advice, and preprogrammed choices that we've absorbed from the day we crawled out of the sandbox and wondered what we would be when we grew up. Whether we're pushed to become doctors or lawyers or to work in the family business, or whether we're informed ("for our own good") that our aspirations are beyond us, all those fears and all that conditioning define our decisions and our expectations without our being aware that it's happening. But it is happening.

That's where we began—on the Assembly Line. The first Roadtrip was forged by a numbing fear that we were locked into preplotted "career" destinations: a doctor, a business consultant, or the next in line to run the family business. None of these options had anything to do with who we really were, but they had everything to do with the expectations we had absorbed. And it filled all of us with a jittery sense of panic. We were afraid we'd wake up one day in high-thread-count, Egyptian cotton sheets in cookie-cutter homes with the devastating realization that we'd been living someone else's dream.

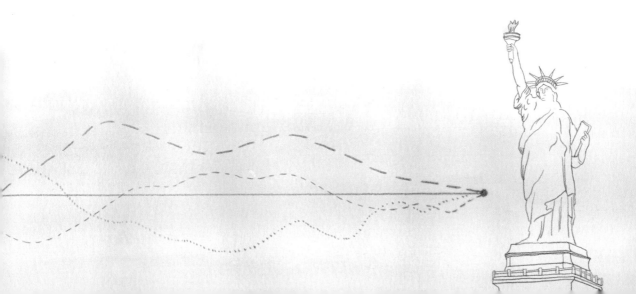

Of course, signing up for the Assembly Line template provides the seductive perceived comfort of safety in numbers. After all, if everyone is making the same few choices, those choices must be the right ones. That's the trickiest part: When you're on the Assembly Line, you often don't even know what your options are. The Assembly Line does the heavy lifting of defining happiness for you; it provides a script to follow, but it's not written for *you* as an individual. The folks we've met on the road, the Leaders—each with their own constellation of interests, experiences, talents, and ambitions—have all discovered ways to change the scripts they were handed.

Rewriting that script can be one of the most difficult acts in your life. It might upset people close to you, it might shake the foundations of your worldview, and it might be scary. The political activist and BET host Jeff Johnson* remembers rejecting the Assembly Line while he was in college on a track scholarship.

As Jeff became more involved in student politics at his school's Black Student Union, his track coach confronted him: "I didn't bring you here for that. I brought you here to go to class and to run track." Jeff's Assembly Line was starkly clear: "star athlete," not "rabble-rousing activist."

Much to his coach's surprise (and his father's anger), Jeff made the tough choice to reject the scholarship so that he could pursue his interests in school with a clear conscience. In rejecting the preprogrammed route, no matter how scary doing so was, Jeff found an important lesson that he continues to share with others.

* **www.roadtripnation.com/leader/jeff-johnson**

"Most people who are successful . . . didn't do what everybody else did. They didn't go the same routes everybody else went. It is the people who think outside the box in whatever discipline they are in who shake the world. No one's looking around at the people who followed a manual saying, 'My God, they followed that manual in a way that was just inspiring.' It is the people who throw the manual away and say there is something beyond this that I can share, or that I can give, or that I can invest, who become successful."

—JEFF JOHNSON, *BET host and political activist*

Being stuck on the Assembly Line often manifests itself as a nagging feeling in your gut that things should be better than they are. That gut feeling is what launches the first phase of your journey. It's time to get to the root of what's causing that anxiety.

Start by asking yourself questions—not just about the road you're already on, but deeply personal questions about who you are and what you want. In short, at this moment, it's time to be selfish. It's time to focus inward to uncover your individuality and to spend some time asking the questions that will reveal what is *authentically* you.

Are you heading toward a destination you really want to reach? Is whatever goal you're striving for worth the work you're putting in? Take some time to think honestly about yourself. Don't think about who you are "supposed" to be, or who your friends think you are, or the persona you've crafted on Facebook or Instagram. Who are you really, right now? Asking these questions of yourself can be a tool for change, both for you and the world at large. It leads to a more honest understanding of what makes you different from others and what unique contribution and perspective you can offer. Don't worry about the answers; think about what questions you *haven't* been asking yourself.

What truly excites me? IF I hAD A hAll PASS On FAiluRE, FEAR, OR . . . whAt wOuld I bE doing?

WHAT WOULD LIFE LOOK LIKE FOR ME TO GET TO THE END AND NOT REGRET DECISIONS I'VE MADE?

When you're on the Assembly Line, those questions can be really challenging. You might be afraid of the answers, or troubled by how far afield you are from where you thought you wanted to be. Or you may find that answering questions about yourself leads to those three frightening words: I don't know.

Don't worry. There's more power in saying "I don't know" than you might think.

WHAT IF AND WHERE TO?

Coasting along on the Assembly Line carries many dangers. One of the most serious is the curse of "what if?," which was hammered home to us by the skiing mogul Pat O'Donnell.* Pat is one of those middle-aged guys who looks ten years younger than he is and exudes energy and a no-frills courage about the pitfalls of life. When we spoke with him, he was the CEO of Aspen Skiing Company; in an earlier incarnation he had effectively invented the Lake Tahoe skiing industry. In an even earlier incarnation, he lived in a tent working as a bellman in Yosemite Valley. Before that, however, Pat was on the Assembly Line.

Pat came from a family of engineers, and his Assembly Line was set: become an engineer. "I went to college and took engineering for one reason only: that's what my father did." Pat hated every minute of his studies, but after college he nevertheless ended up working in San Francisco in the family profession. Pat was stuck on a line that didn't speak to whom he really was or what he really wanted. And so, in his late twenties, Pat leapt off the Assembly Line.

*   **www.roadtripnation.com/leader/pat-o-donnell**

"I was twenty-seven, by then really floundering and probably not happy in my heart," recalls Pat, "and my interest at that time was rock climbing in Yosemite Valley, so I would drive all night Friday, climb all weekend, and then begrudgingly go back to work." And then Pat decided life was too short to spend all his time working a job he hated and living for the weekends. He left engineering and took a low-level job as a park employee at Yosemite, rock climbing in his off hours and sleeping under the stars.

"I followed my heart and my values system; six years in Yosemite, and then I said I gotta go." From Yosemite he ended up in Tahoe, helping to build one of the first ski resorts in the region. And then Pat leapt again, landing closer to where he wanted to be, crafting new and better iterations of himself, from Tahoe to Aspen.

"In retrospect, it's easy, but at the time I was petrified," Pat says about one of his many leaps. And although he longed for a sure thing, he knew he had to follow his gut. **The real security blanket is your values and your vision. If it's not working for you, move. Every day is a wasted day after that."**

In lieu of following the Assembly Line, Pat asked "what if?" at the right time—that time being as soon and as often as possible. Pat knew that one day, "You wake up and you're sick, or you're old, and you say 'what if?'" He turned "what if?" from a question of regret to a triumph. Taking those two simple words seriously is what nudged him off the Assembly Line.

There can be any number of self-created reasons for staying on your own Assembly Line, and they don't have to be bad, by any definition. There's nothing wrong with wanting security and a steady paycheck. There's nothing wrong with wanting the house with a view or a healthy 401(k). The danger arises when you haven't asked questions about why you're doing what you're doing and striving for what you're striving for.

So let's ask some questions about why—starting with, where are you headed?

The Assembly Line of _____.

(your name)

The voices around me are saying

"I should be a _____."

"I have to_____ ."

And if I stay on this Assembly Line . . .

Five years from now I will be _____.

(busy, lost, afraid, excited, curious, employed)

Is my job interesting?

Do I live for the weekends?

Am I having fun?

Who is with me along the way?

. . . and in ten years, I will be _____.

(struggling, having fun, afraid, working hard, building, off track, tired, excited)

Am I good at what I do?

Am I challenged?

Do I feel like I'm going somewhere?

Is there momentum in my life?

Do I have a wife/husband/partner? Kids?

Am I happy?

Am I where I thought I would be?

Am I playing as much as I hope to?

. . . and in fifteen years, I will be _____ .

(happy, confused, afraid, excited, stuck, accomplished, proud, regretful)

Where will I live?

What does my work look like?

Do I like the people I spend time with?

Does the work I do give me pleasure and meaning?

Am I a better person than I was fifteen years ago?

Am I proud of how I've lived life thus far?

Are the answers you've given to these questions freaking you out?

YES

NO

We felt the same way.
And just as it was for us, this
is a great place to start.
Keep reading.

The road ahead looks pretty good.
You're one of the fortunate ones.
Keep reading. This book should
confirm what you're thinking and
help you stay on your own road.

Taking risks in your life and stepping off the Assembly Line will not, as we've been told to believe, automatically lead to your new cardboard-box home under the freeway.

So many of the people we've interviewed and been inspired by, the folks we refer to as Leaders, found true success, both financially and psychologically, after years of being stalled on the Assembly Line. They broke free from the Line by asking the big, embarrassing questions, the touchy-feely new-agey kind of questions that can seem like they have nothing to do with the predicament you hope to solve. But asking "Who am I?" will instantly slow down the wheels of the Assembly Line. The slower the Line, the easier it will be to jump off.

Judge Penny Brown Reynolds* puts it simply: "Tapping into your purpose takes a great deal of discipline, because you have to ask yourself the question every day when you open your eyes: 'Who am I?'" Penny grew up in poverty in Louisiana, overcoming homelessness and abuse before she got to law school. This step was enough to showcase Penny as someone who didn't take the path laid out for her, but what's amazing is that Penny has never stopped questioning her choices and path to make sure they still align with her interests. For Penny, her road was about helping people fight oppression and abuse. She became a judge, presided over a television show courtroom, and now is an ordained minister, all in the name of following her own road. She sums it up: "I know now in my heart my road is constantly evolving—that it's about keeping your heart open. Stop watching your life from the sidelines."

Learning what you don't know about yourself will reveal the ways in which the path you're on diverges from the path you will ultimately want to take. As you question the road ahead, the gears of your personal Assembly Line will start to rattle and slow. It's time to leap.

  www.roadtripnation.com/leader/penny-brown-reynolds

CHAPTER 2

SHED THE NOISE

The whirling cacophony of voices, advice, and expectations that drowns out our individual expression is the Noise. It comes from family, teachers and counselors, and society at large. It comes from marketing campaigns and all the endless stuff that we're told to buy; it's embedded in every celebrity-endorsed product, and smiling at us from every glossy magazine cover. It can come with equal force from friends or rivals and from strangers or family. It's in the books we read and the TV shows we watch, it's all over our social media spheres, and most dangerously, it's within ourselves. For some of us, the Noise might remind us to make money above all else, or to follow in the footsteps of a successful sibling. For others, it might insist that we'll never be good enough to make it in a chosen pursuit, or that we'd be crazy to try something different from other people. Whatever the case, the Noise is the furnace that drives your personal Assembly Line.

Different as it is for each of us, the Noise is also everybody's starting point. Virtually every Leader we've spoken to on the road has described the Noise, in one form or another, factoring into their lives.

"My family did not want me to be a teacher. My mother said, 'You're never going to make any money!'"

—*Tracey Parrish, former teacher and senior marketing manager for the AT&T Foundry*

"When I was a senior in high school [at a Catholic boarding school], two days before my graduation I was told by this nun, 'Get a good job pumping gas in a gas station and stick with it. That's your life.'"

—*Gerard Baker, first Native American superintendent of Mount Rushmore National Memorial*

"Because of where I grew up, the Jewish suburbs of Baltimore, you were expected to prepare yourself to go to medical school . . . what else would I do? That's what people did if they were smart: they became doctors!"

—*Ira Glass, host of* This American Life

"I had a very traditional family; girls didn't go away to school. You just stayed in the house until you were married. . . . I came home and said, 'I've been accepted to the University of Florida.' They said, 'Tú estás loca?!'"

—*Betty Cortina-Weiss, editorial director of* Latina *magazine*

"I was accepted to the USC music school as a violin performance major, but on the first day of school I decided to change my major to jazz and my parents freaked out . . . all these people who had nurtured me suddenly didn't want to talk to me anymore . . . I wanted to combine the traditional with the new, but was taught by classical people that you can't mix the two."

—Paul Dateh, hip-hop violinist

"I went to a prep school, and I remember telling one of my teachers I was gonna play drums at this gig, and he said [sarcastically], 'Oh, nice use of your education. . . .' It was really discouraging because he didn't see drumming as valid in any way."

—Chris Wink, cofounder of Blue Man Group

"My community is in poverty, mostly farm workers. My parents worked in the fields, and they don't have a high school education. . . . When I was in high school there were some folks who told me to pick up a trade, and not pursue my dream of furthering my education because I would fail."

—Raul Ruiz, physician, congressman, and first Latino to earn three graduate degrees from Harvard University

"I went home and said, 'Mom, I wanna learn how to surf!' And she answered, 'Absolutely not. Surfing is for boys. You need to be sitting on the beach in a bikini, not out there competing with them. You're never going to get a boyfriend that way.'"

—Holly Beck, professional surfer

What should strike you about the Noise in these examples is that it's not necessarily malicious. For the most part, it's just well-meaning advice, blanketed by good intentions and persuasive through its persistence. The trick becomes distinguishing the Noise from genuinely helpful guidance. We can all agree that advice from peers and elders is an essential way to fact-check yourself and gain insight about your road, but we've also all been subject to boilerplate wisdom that doesn't take into account who we are as individuals, and that advice isn't helpful—it's just the Noise.

Adding to the danger is that the Noise can also give us a way to avoid our fears and insecurities. Listening to what we "should do" can make us feel like we have our very own "emergency parachute." The perceived security of groupthink keeps you insulated. If you're simply following a preconstructed path, you're not to blame when the path runs afoul or doesn't turn out the way you'd been told it would. The parachute of the Noise doesn't, of course, provide any real safety; it only keeps you from examining how your day-to-day decisions have brought you this moment and this identity. It keeps you from facing your doubts. But examining the root of those doubts will open up new ways to discover who you really are.

The Oscar-nominated filmmaker Richard Linklater* describes overcoming the Noise as akin to ordering a meal that's not on the menu. Growing up in a small town in Texas, he remembers wanting to be a writer. But his desire to enter the arts was met with prickly disapproval. "It was, 'Well, yeah, you could study literature, but you'll never achieve anything. I mean, we don't do that.'"

  www.roadtripnation.com/leader/richard-linklater

The menu in front of Richard was pretty clear. Take a safe route, get a law degree, scrap the arts. "And that's just the practical advice that your loved ones, the people closest to you, will give you," Richard says. "Everyone around me was saying 'You should go to medical school, you should go to law school.' Do they really want you to be a lawyer? No. It just sounds good. I remember thinking, 'Anything everyone wants to do can't be right. I don't want to live like them. I don't want their life."

Richard chose to rebel against the path in front of him. As his fellow twenty-something friends committed to graduate school and off-the-rack careers, he made a different choice. "I remember just sitting there going, 'Okay, I'm gonna reject the advice and do the complete polar opposite of what everyone's telling me to do. I don't know where that'll leave me, but my hunch is it'll be a much more interesting place than had I followed everyone's advice.'"

Richard went to work on an oil rig, saving as much money as he could so that, after a couple of years, he was able to enter what he calls a "monkish, dropout, total-devotion phase." He ravenously ingested everything he could about film-making. He watched ungodly amounts of movies, read books, bought editing equipment (and taught himself how to use it), and cultivated his skills. Success for Richard was never a foregone conclusion, but with his inner voice guiding him through the many setbacks and challenges he faced, and no shortage of hard work, Richard has become one of the most critically acclaimed independent filmmakers in the business, making such lauded films as *Dazed and Confused* and *Before Sunset*.

43

Let's return to BET host Jeff Johnson from the last chapter. He's the college track star who rejected a scholarship so he could pursue his interest in helping others. Having been there himself, he knows the powerful difference between making intentional choices and just floating along on what he calls the "remote control life"—avoiding decisions that would push your life in authentic and inspiring directions. "Young people are destroying their calling in the name of satisfying what their parents were unable to do." The questions you have to ask yourself are: Who's pressing the buttons in your life? Are you compromising what you believe about yourself in order to fit into a precast mold? Or are you the one in control, making choices based on your own interests, values, hopes, and dreams? Jeff reminds us, **"Whether people agree or disagree with you, so what? They don't have to live your life."**

When we first began speaking about the Noise at public events, we got a lot of flak. Teachers would quietly take us aside. Parents would stand up in the middle of our presentations feeling threatened, saying: "Let me see if I'm getting this straight. Are you telling our kids not to listen to their parents and teachers? Because I've got a problem with that." To them we'd say that rejecting the Noise isn't about shutting everyone out like a rebellious teen who's hell-bent on getting a face tattoo, parents be damned! Rather, it's about taking an honest look at the influences, expectations, and constructive criticism in your life and making informed decisions. Sometimes the critics are right. Sure, in a perfect world, everything we do would warrant high fives and gold stars from our moms, bosses, and random people on the street, but we have to accept that our missteps will be numerous and difficult to notice when we're in the thick of it.

Even Joe Rogan, the combative comedian and erstwhile inducer of reality TV insect consumption, concedes that sometimes criticism can be the best medicine. "There is no criticism like internet criticism," Joe says. "When those creeps are anonymous, sitting behind their computers, they can say the nastiest things ever! But sometimes they're right. That's when it's really difficult: when someone's a huge jerk, but what they're saying is valid."

STUDY YOURSELF

How can you distinguish between negative Noise and useful feedback?

You filter it by being honest with yourself. When Richard Linklater decided to do his contrarian swing away from all the advice he was receiving about his life, it wasn't that he was able to immediately replace it with a clear vision of what he wanted. But he did know that the conventional spiel wasn't connecting with basic truths about himself. This awareness of the expectations Richard had for his life led him to take a self-reflective step away from the Noise. To get to that self-reflective step, you need to start studying yourself. Unearth your true interests, values, and aspirations in order to see how the Noise is inconsistent with your individuality. Test out the suggestions, advice, and assumptions you've absorbed and think about whether they harmonize with your interests and values or are a product of external expectations that you don't subscribe to.

When it comes to criticism, constructive or destructive, it helps to simply picture your teachers', parents', friends', family's, and coworkers' remarks as comments under the YouTube video of your life. It doesn't matter how many "likes" their comments may get; it's up to *you* to decide whether their words are valid and worthy of deeper consideration.

The basic rule is: If the message you're hearing takes into account who you are as an individual, and it rings true, chances are it isn't the Noise. If the message raises that gut-churning feeling of "This is not me," it's the Noise. The great thing about pinpointing the discrepancies between your authentic self and the clamor of the Noise is it will help solidify your value system, which in turn helps you more clearly identify new Noise when it comes down the pike.

Want to try this out? Play with the flowchart. Reflect on your day, your week, or even the past year. What comments, advice, and feedback did you receive from others? Was it Noise? Punch your findings through the flowchart. As the data drops through, you should, as with a sort of psychological coin sorter, end up with a big, heaping pile of Noise in the Noise column.

Write down all that Noise somewhere—on the next page, in a journal or a notebook, or on a mirror. Take a "before" photo of your Noise so you have a reference to look back on. It's time to destroy it.

Erase it! Burn it! Smash it to bits! Attach it to a brick and drop it into the sea, send it into orbit—whatever method of destruction feels best to you. Take an "after" photo, or record a video of the whole experience. If you'd like, upload it wherever you share and tag it **#RoadmapBook**. Search the hashtag and check out other people's Noise-smashing.

What you've just done is create distance between yourself and the Noise. This is crucial, because if you don't flush it out, the Noise will infiltrate your psyche. It will work its way into your thoughts like a parasite, manipulating you just as the *Dicrocoelium dendriticum* larvae mind-controls an ant to latch onto the tip of a grass blade and stay there all night until a cow or sheep eats it (look it up— it's creepy!). Your uncle's gentle chiding that you're "just not cut out for that" will slowly morph into "I'm just not cut out for that." **Internalized Noise affects our belief systems and erodes our sense of self, killing our confidence and dreams. Then we pass that corrupt view of the world on to others like a bad cold.**

IS IT NOISE?

" _____ "

_____

Write an example of your Noise here.

Does this comment take your own
individuality into account?

| YES | | NO |

YES → Is it valid?

NO → Do you trust this
person's opinion?

| YES | NO | | NO | YES |

This is constructive criticism.
What should you be taking
into account?

_____

_____

_____

Is there some truth
to this comment?

| NO | YES |

This is Noise but there might
be something to learn from it.
Can you think of anything?

_____

_____

_____

THIS IS NOISE.
SHED IT.

Elaine Kwon,* a celebrated concert pianist, five-time U.S. Tae Kwon Do champion, and music-theory lecturer at MIT, is not—by outward appearances—someone whose life has been dominated by the Noise. But the fight against self-doubt is something she has dealt with her entire adult life.

"My father just wanted us to succeed," says Elaine. "He said, 'Not only are you Asian and a minority, but you're also female, so you have to work doubly hard and be doubly better.' It was really tough when it came time to make a decision about college, and what I was supposed to do. I was supposed to become a medical doctor. My parents had a vision of me being stable and secure and having a nice profession."

Think about that for a moment. How do you fight against that vision, coming from someone you love? It seems perfectly reasonable. How could you not absorb it into your own vision—even if it goes against your core values? Elaine's struggle with the Noise manifested as a struggle with self-doubt about what she really wanted out of life.

Elaine had to choose between fulfilling her parents' expectations and chasing her own dream of becoming a pianist. She faced a crucial challenge. "I was already set up to go to University of Washington and enroll in pre-med. But I just didn't want to go into medicine," she recalls. "So I had a very tough conversation with my father. And I just decided, I'm going to follow my heart. Because otherwise I'm gonna feel sick inside. So I didn't listen. I went into music."

The massiveness of this choice is powerful, and it's something Elaine probably understands only in hindsight. "If I had just followed the regular path, I probably wouldn't be playing at Carnegie Hall right now," she told us.

  www.roadtripnation.com/leader/elaine-kwon

But Elaine's story holds another, perhaps more important lesson. Elaine's struggle against internal Noise is not a long-resolved struggle from her college years. "I felt so much pressure," Elaine says, "and I still feel that pressure. But it's mostly, myself . . . It's mostly—" Here Elaine pauses, as if realizing something for the first time—"Maybe, maybe it's a habit from when I was a kid. . . . The pressure comes externally and then, I internalize it, and now I still put pressure on myself."

There it is. There is no lifelong vaccination against the Noise. It sucks for us, but, like distressed denim or tax day, it is never wholly banished. That might sound like a grim pronouncement to end this chapter on, but it's actually comforting.

Consider the Noise an equalizer. Every successful person, from rulers of nations to innovative engineers to mustachioed cocktail mixologists, has to overcome the Noise. Every day. Before our Roadtrips, we didn't imagine that successful people from all walks of life struggled with the same doubts that afflicted us, but hearing the stories of others helped normalize our own struggles. We—and you—are not alone, even if the struggle never ends. Want proof? Here's a glimpse at our internal monologue when we were first writing this:

Is this chapter working? Does it make sense? Are we smart enough to be writing this book?

CHAPTER 3

BUILD A LIFE, NOT A RÉSUMÉ

What defines you as a person? What have you done, what do you do now, and what will you do that makes you who you are?

When you think about these questions, we'd wager that the last thing that comes to mind is the résumé you're tinkering with. Yet the paycheck-to-paycheck world we're brought up in has taught us to focus on that piece of paper as the key to happiness and success. "Will this look good on my résumé?" we ask ourselves when faced with crucial life decisions.

Where, on the balance sheet of skills, accomplishments, and career history, can we codify our actions in a way that will impress the next HR director who happens to open our email with "Résumé Attached" in the subject line? Such is the dilemma facing the modern résumé builder. Like the video store, the résumé builder is a relic of an earlier age, slowly being outpaced by a new breed—the self-constructors and job-inventors. But this fact hasn't reached those in charge. So we continue to go through the motions as we've been taught. We dutifully seek life paths that have very little to do with who we are— and a lot to do with what *appears* to be successful.

"On your tombstone at the end of the day, they're gonna see three things: your birth date, that dash, and your death date. The thing that has the most importance to me is that dash. . . . What happened in your life during the time you were born to the time you passed away? What defines you as a person?"

—**GREGORY CARROLL**, *CEO, American Jazz Museum*

Gregory's question gets to the core of any act of Self-Construction. A résumé will never be the answer to "What defines you as a person?" It won't stand in as the dash that separates your birth date and your death date. Résumé building that is divorced from any exploration of what truly fulfills and excites you will lead to unhappy consequences. Maybe it's a high-paying rat-race job that finds you surrounded by superficial jerks working seventy-two-hour weeks for no particularly good reason, or maybe it's an unfulfilling "stepping stone" job that doesn't seem to be doing much stepping toward anything meaningful. When that brass-ring job is neither stimulating, nourishing, nor congruent with our interests, we can get stuck in the working-for-the-weekend, *Office Space* mentality. There's a reason that situation is so justly satirized: because it sucks.

Obviously nobody sets out to find a job they hate, but in accepting the Noise and following the Assembly Line, many of us inadvertently end up there, living in service of a résumé—which is crazy. Think about it in terms of pure hours. A third of your life will be spent at work, and much of the rest of it will be spent sleeping (ah, sweet sleep, eases the pain!). Which comes out to eight hours a day, five days a week, fifty-two weeks a year (minus two weeks' vacation), and if you keep it up you'll be doing it for roughly forty-five years. So that's . . .

90,

hours of your life wasted at

000

a job that you can't stand

All in the service of what? Paying the bills. Which of course has to get done, but if we've learned anything in our decade-plus on the road, it's that there is truly more than one way to get there. Financial security and an engaging, satisfying Worklife are not mutually exclusive. In fact, our experience shows that they go hand in hand.

So let's kill the résumé—well, at least philosophically speaking. What we mean is, let's kill the life that's led by a résumé. The best résumés don't showcase all the "right" steps and benchmarks. They showcase someone who is engaged and excited by the world and actively pursuing their interests. And if you're busy doing that, you're probably not, well, building your résumé. You're building a life.

When you build a life, you end up building a good résumé.

THE DEFERRED-LIFE PLAN

Instead of trying to craft a résumé that showcases you as an ambitious, hard-working problem-solver, go out there and *be* ambitious, solve problems, and work hard, all in the name of what interests and excites you. **Don't wait to do what you really want to.** You don't want to live your life in the waiting room. When we sat down with author and technology executive Randy Komisar,* he called this mode of living the "deferred-life plan."

The deferred-life plan, as Randy describes it in his book *The Monk and the Riddle,* is a two-step dance of avoidance. First, you do what you have to, then you do what you want to. Go become a lawyer because it looks good and will pay well, then, maybe, when you retire, you can pursue what you really want to do. There are countless less extreme versions of this conundrum—even being a weekend warrior is a deferred-life plan. Let's get back to the hours again, which are the

  www.roadtripnation.com/leader/randy-komisar

only real commodity you possess. If you're only living for the 48 hours of the weekend, how do you value the other 120 hours spent Monday through Friday?

Randy can attest to the perils of the deferred-life plan firsthand. A successful author, Randy helped launch TiVo, served as CEO of LucasArts, and is a partner at a venture capital firm that has backed cutting-edge tech companies such as Zynga, WebMD, and Nest. Right out of college he continually followed his interests, from community-development programs to concert promotion, but after a while he needed to get serious and started to play the game of doing what you hate in the service of a perceived future outcome.

In his twenties, Randy enrolled in law school but found no joy in studying law or in his day-to-day work as a lawyer. "I had this fear that I had gained something by being a lawyer and I had something to lose by not being a lawyer. The norm is to fall into that sort of way of thinking."

"The problem with the deferred-life plan," Randy explains, "is that even if you succeed at it, you gotta then figure out what the heck you want to do. And what's important is understanding what [mindset] is yours and what is society's. The faster you come to grips with that, the more likely you are to find satis-faction." Despite being at the pinnacle of résumé-worthy success (a lawyer at Apple! Hot shit!), Randy yearned to use his talents in other ways.

So he abandoned the safe route and reinvented himself as a virtual CEO for companies in technology and entertainment, slowly but surely carving out his niche as a creative free agent. By backing creative businesses and writing books, his impact on the world around him (and his satisfaction level) became far greater. Randy's résumé ended up looking way better than it would have if he had just followed the safe résumé-builder approach to life.

Randy gave up his deferred-life plan in favor of living what he loves now, today. But not all are so fortunate. We all know people who adhere to the "suffer now, enjoy later" concept. Heck, maybe your parents bought into it, and they're just itching to finally take that garden design class or Greek isles trip they've been talking about forever. The concept certainly hits close to home for us at Roadtrip Nation, largely because we've spent so many hours traversing the territory Randy's talking about. We don't mean when we're out doing presentations or producing the public television series. We're talking about our experience with the RV culture in the United States. Don't get us wrong; we're not judging RVers. They're our people! But to say we stand out among them would be an understatement. Every road we take, every campsite, truck stop, rest stop we sleep at, we get sideways looks. This isn't only because our RV is fluorescent green and 99.99 percent of the other RVs have signed some sort of secret pact to stick to the same color spectrum of beige, with the occasional mural of a tiger, or a wolf, or an eagle sitting on top of a wolf perched on a cliff overlooking a river and a tiger . . . (Sorry, fell down the rabbit hole there for a second.)

The point is, not only do we stand out visibly; there's something else subtly going on here. There's a palpable air among many of the RVers we encounter that silently communicates: "You kids shouldn't be out here. You haven't earned this yet." And viewed in the context of the deferred-life plan, it seems like their attitude is part of the whole Noise message, the defensive societal struggle to keep the world the same.

We can sympathize. They've spent years slaving away at this or that. Post-poning. And it was all for this moment, this trip! And here we are, appearing like a ragtag group of wayward youth, green to the "real world." Bet they wouldn't be too impressed with our résumés, either. But this is a perfect metaphor for the residual effects of the old way of thinking. The traditional career template, which is increasingly obsolete, still dictates the way we act, dress, format our accomplishments on a piece of paper, and chase the job that makes the most amount of money so someday, decades from now, we can afford to retire, buy an RV, and do the very thing we're actually doing at the moment . . . living our lives the way we want. Remember, there is no guarantee of a certain future waiting for you, even if you do everything right.

FORGET WORK-LIFE BALANCE. INTEGRATE!

There is a paradigm shift happening in the way work and life are approached. Well-meaning social scientists have been bandying about terms like "work-life balance" as a solution for people stuck on the Assembly Line, and CEOs have been lapping it up and dispensing it in their memos and all-hands meetings like it's gospel. But we think work-life balance is a sham. Work-life balance implies two separate and opposing points that need to orbit about each other. *A sacrifice must be made somewhere. Either follow what truly motivates you or put food on the table.* In order to balance the two, we toil away at jobs that don't fulfill us, and then, if we have the energy, we cram a few hours of pursuing our genuine interests into our evenings while we juggle cooking dinner, getting our clothes into the washer, and maintaining some semblance of a normal relationship with a significant other, friends, and family. Hardly a balance, right? Which is why, worn down by the losing game of work-life balance, most of us just choose to collapse on the couch and watch hours of terrible TV at the end of the day.

But "real living" doesn't have to be the few hours after quitting time when you cram in the things you actually like to do. With the right intention and mindset, you can feed and clothe yourself *by* pursuing work you believe in. What we're talking about is not work-life balance, but work-life integration— the incorporation of your interests into your work. Imagine waking up every day energized to be doing what you're doing at work that day. That's Worklife. One word, not two. It doesn't mean you won't still want to blow it off and go back to bed, but when you do stop hitting the snooze button, you're not filled with dread as you start your day. We've seen this demonstrated over and over with the people we've interviewed. Sometimes they did it from the get-go, sometimes it was a midlife shift, and sometimes they struggled throughout their entire careers to figure it out. But we wouldn't be writing this book if we didn't have proof that it is in fact possible to live with integrity and authenticity in the pursuit of meaningful work built on deep personal interests while still paying the bills.

Mountaineer and nature photographer Jimmy Chin* is another extreme example, but in his story, we see how intentional decisions motivated by interest can get you to fantastic places. As an expedition photographer who snaps photos for clients like *National Geographic*, The North Face, Patagonia, and Rolex, Jimmy has the kind of gig people envy—explore the world, take photos, go skiing, and get paid. But what is powerful in Jimmy's story is that he didn't come from a background that empowered him to take the risks he did to build his career.

  www.roadtripnation.com/leader/jimmy-chin

He just took them. Before beginning a traditional post-college path toward business or law school, he convinced his parents he needed a year to explore the world and himself. In Europe, the notion of a "gap year" (often between high school and college) is common for just this sort of exploration. Here in the states, Jimmy had to force his own gap year. And that gap year became seven years of living in the back of a beat-up Subaru. Jimmy did odd jobs that others wouldn't dare waste valuable "résumé space" on, as he skied, climbed mountains, and took photos. He wasn't living in a car because he was lazy, but because he wanted to intentionally pursue what was important to him on his own terms, devoting his limited resources to his interests. "When you do something like that," he says, "it goes against the grain of everything you've been brought up to think."

But those intentional choices started to work in Jimmy's favor in unexpected ways. One gorgeous photo sold to a magazine led to another, and another, and then in a few years, Jimmy was leading some of the most daunting photography expeditions ever attempted, capturing breathtaking moments, from the sandstone towers of Mali to the peak of Mount Kilimanjaro.

For Jimmy, once he found what he loved most, one thing led to the next. "All these little stepping stones kind of just led me to all these different places. In some ways, I don't feel like I ever had control of my life. But I would throw myself at climbing. And climbing produced photography. And also out of climbing, I put together complex expeditions to really remote places. And I couldn't have done that without my education. You pick up skills that you don't even know you have in college. And then all of a sudden you begin to apply different things that you've picked up."

Like Randy (and like so many of the other Leaders we've met), Jimmy used what he had already learned, integrated it into his interests, and built a life that translated into a stellar résumé. But the life was the goal, not the piece of paper.

It all comes down to how you spend your limited time on Earth—to that dash on the tombstone between your birth and death dates. How will you define yourself as a person, how do you add genuine meaning to the space between the two dates on your tombstone?

The best advice: start now and act with intention. If you're young, explore and pursue your interests while you're likely more free of overarching responsibilities like family and finances. If you're older, you can still do it, you just might need to be a little more strategic. Regardless of where you are or where you start, the skills, experiences, and expertise you gain along the way will give you much more pride in the "dash" that is your life . . . and what ultimately shows up on your résumé.

Spend some time thinking about how you can begin the integration of your work and interests, and how they each exist in your life now. Will your time here on Earth be spent working on something that gives you meaning? Building skills so you can do more of what you love?

What will fill your "dash?"

Jot down anything and everything you envision for a life well lived, according to *you*.

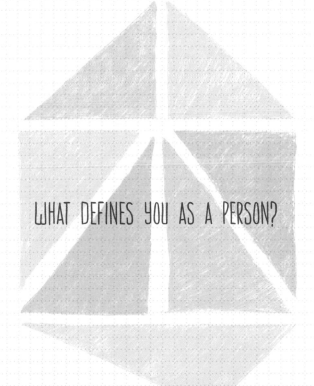

WHAT DEFINES YOU AS A PERSON?

RIGHT OR LEFT?

By Zachariah Cowan

IT WAS AN UNHOLY 115°F/46°C AS WE CAME BUSTING THROUGH THE DESERT, SWEATING THROUGH OUR SHIRTS, STARING STRAIGHT INTO THE WHITE HEAT AHEAD ON OUR WAY TO OUR NEXT INTERVIEW. WHILE IDLING AT A ROADSIDE GAS STATION WE WERE GREETED BY A TARANTULA THE SIZE OF MY HAND, SLINKING PAST THE PUMPS AS IF TO SIMULTANEOUSLY WELCOME ALL THE PASSERSBY TO HIS TERRITORY AND REMIND THEM THAT THEY'RE NOT HOME ANYMORE.

WELCOME TO ARIZONA.

OUR PLANNED ROUTE WOULD TAKE US FARTHER SOUTH, CROSSING THE RIO GRANDE AND INTO EL PASO, BUT I KNEW THERE'D BE NO RESPITE FROM THE HEAT. SO IN A WAY I WAS THANKFUL THAT OUR NEXT INTERVIEW WAS PLANNED FOR EARLY THE FOLLOWING MORNING, AT WHAT I HOPED WOULD BE A SLIGHTLY LESS BLISTERING 7:00 A.M.

OUR INTERVIEW WAS WITH DEON CLARK, AND WE WERE TO MEET HIM AT THE PALO VERDE NUCLEAR GENERATING STATION, THE LARGEST NUCLEAR ENERGY FACILITY IN THE UNITED STATES, GENERATING ELECTRICITY FOR FOUR MILLION PEOPLE IN THE

Zachariah Cowan is a bundle of inquisitive energy from Columbus, Ohio. Captivated by everything from sustainable agriculture to blacksmithing, he followed his love of sciences to a major in geology at Ohio State University. But even with that direction, Zachariah had difficulty funneling his varied interests into one concrete pursuit. He joined two other Roadtrippers in our Green RV on a cross-country search for ways to turn his interests into a meaningful livelihood.

SOUTHWEST. WAKING UP AT THE LOCAL TRUCK STOP WHERE WE HAD SLEPT THE NIGHT BEFORE, I COULD SEE THE STEAM RISING FROM THE SPACE-STATION LIKE STRUCTURE ON THE HORIZON. AFTER A BIRD BATH IN THE GAS STATION SINK, I GRABBED A CUP OF COFFEE FOR DEON AND WE HEADED TO MEET HIM.

DEON IS A BIG GUY WHO GREW UP ON THE SOUTH SIDE OF CHICAGO. HE HAS THAT EX-MILITARY LOOK, ALL POSTURE AND MUSCLE, BUT TEMPERED WITH A GENEROUS DEMEANOR AND A WELCOMING SMILE. WE SPENT THE MORNING WITH DEON AS HE TOLD US ABOUT HIS HARDSCRABBLE YOUTH, WITH A FATHER WHO WAS MORE OR LESS MIA HIS WHOLE LIFE AND FAMILY MEMBERS FLOATING IN AND OUT OF JAIL—AN ALL TOO COMMON STORY LINE IN HIS NEIGHBORHOOD.

HE HAD GOTTEN OUT OF THE SOUTH SIDE BY JOINING THE NAVY. "I WAS SEVENTEEN WHEN I WENT IN," DEON TOLD US. "FRESH OUT OF HIGH SCHOOL, AND THE NAVY'S PROGRAM WAS SET UP THAT IN EIGHTEEN MONTHS YOU WENT FROM KNOW-NOTHING TO QUALIFIED TO OPERATE A NAVAL NUCLEAR POWER PLANT. EIGHTEEN MONTHS! FIFTEEN HOURS A DAY, MONDAY THROUGH MONDAY. NO WEEKENDS, NO BREAKS."

BY AGE NINETEEN, DEON WAS LEADING A CREW OF FORTY-TWO TECHNICIANS ON A NUCLEAR AIRCRAFT CARRIER. "THAT'S THE PART THAT I LOVED ABOUT IT. YOU BECOME A VALUABLE ASSET

TO ANYONE IN ANY INSTITUTION BECAUSE OF THAT KNOWLEDGE."
HIS NAVAL EXPERIENCE LED TO LUCRATIVE WORK IN THE CORPORATE
SECTOR OF NUCLEAR ENGINEERING.

THAT UP-BY-THE-BOOTSTRAPS STORY ALONE PROBABLY WOULD'VE
BEEN ENOUGH TO BRING US OUT TO THE DESERT TO VISIT HIM, BUT
DEON'S TALE GETS EVEN MORE COMPELLING. IT BEGAN WHEN THE
ADULT DEON WENT BACK TO THE SOUTH SIDE ON A VISIT TO HIS MOM.
"IT WAS SEEING THIS SENSE OF HOPELESSNESS. SO I STARTED VOLUN-
TEERING A LOT OF MY TIME WHERE I WOULD GO TO DIFFERENT HIGH
SCHOOLS AND JUST TALK TO STUDENTS AND SHARE MY STORY. I WOULD
FIND THAT THESE YOUNG PEOPLE WANTED TO KNOW: HOW DID I DO IT?"

DEON USED HIS LIFE SAVINGS TO FOUND THE LEGACY INITIATIVE,
A NON-PROFIT WHOSE GOAL IS TO FOSTER OPPORTUNITIES IN UNDER-
SERVED COMMUNITIES. THIS WAS POSSIBLE BECAUSE OF HIS FOCUSED
DETERMINATION TO MASTER A SKILL. WHEN YOU GROW UP AS DEON
DID, THE IDEA OF SECURITY AND SAFETY TAKES ON A DEEPER
MEANING. HIS ADVICE TO US:

> **"The military's training caused me to become
> very, very useful in the corporate nuclear
> world. My advice is to lock in on a skill, and
> master it, such that now you've got something
> to fall back on."**

I'D HEARD THIS KIND OF THING BEFORE. THE OLD FALLBACK
PLAN THAT MANY PARENTS AND COUNSELORS USE TO CHECK OUR
DREAMS. THAT KIND OF STATEMENT IS VERY OFTEN AND VERY EASILY
TRANSMUTED INTO THE NOISE. BUT COMING FROM DEON, IT FELT
DIFFERENT, REAL IN A POWERFUL WAY—DEON HAD LIVED IT AND
EARNED IT. DEON'S FALLBACK WAS AN INTENTIONALLY DEVELOPED
SET OF SPECIALIZED SKILLS THAT SPOKE TO HIS NATURAL TALENTS.
IT MEANS HE HAS A SIX-FIGURE SALARY WITHIN HIS GRASP WHENEVER
HE NEEDS IT. AND IT GAVE HIM THE FREEDOM TO FUND HIS NON-
PROFIT AND MAKE A POSITIVE IMPACT ON OTHER PEOPLE'S LIVES.

WE SAID OUR GOOD-BYES AND CLIMBED BACK INTO THE RV. WE DROVE EAST IN SILENCE, EACH OF US LOST IN THOUGHT AS WE WRESTLED WITH THE IMPLICATIONS OF DEON'S STORY. DID I HAVE, IN MY OWN LIFE, SOMETHING LIKE WHAT DEON HAD? A PURPOSEFUL FALLBACK? DID I HAVE THE GUTS AND DRIVE TO LIVE LIKE DEON? AND IF I DID WHAT WOULD I DO WITH IT?

OUR NEXT STOP WAS COLUMBUS, NEW MEXICO, POPULATION 1,664, BUT WITH OUR RV CAMPED OUT ON COLUMBUS'S DESERTED MAIN DRAG, WE WOULD'VE GUESSED IT TO BE MORE LIKE 25. MAYBE 50, TOPS. WITH ITS ROW OF LOW-SLUNG STOREFRONTS SILENT UNDER THE MOONLIGHT, IT FELT LIKE A TOWN OUT OF *THE LAST PICTURE SHOW*. WITH NO PICTURE SHOW OF ANY KIND TO DIVERT US, WE KICKED ROCKS AROUND ON THE STREET TO PASS THE TIME UNTIL WE KILLED THE LIGHTS AND SETTLED INTO THE CREAKS AND SWAYS THAT COME WITH SLEEPING IN AN RV.

WE WERE THERE TO MEET PAUL SALOPEK. PAUL IS A TWO-TIME PULITZER PRIZE–WINNING JOURNALIST WHO HAS WRITTEN FOR *NATIONAL GEOGRAPHIC* MAGAZINE AND THE *CHICAGO TRIBUNE*, AMONG MANY OTHER PUBLICATIONS. HOW HAD THIS GLOBE-TROTTING REPORTER ENDED UP IN WHAT SEEMED LIKE THE MIDDLE OF NOWHERE, A STONE'S THROW FROM THE MEXICAN BORDER? BY CHOICE? BY ACCIDENT? WHAT LED HIM TO THIS TINY CORNER OF THE COUNTRY?

PAUL WAS A RAMBLER IN HIS YOUTH, AND IN MANY WAYS HE STILL IS. ONE SUMMER, AFTER GRADUATING WITH A BIOLOGY DEGREE, PAUL WAS CROSSING THE COUNTRY ON A MOTORCYCLE, WITH THE END GOAL OF SHIPPING OUT ON A SHRIMP BOAT IN THE GULF. BUT THEN, IN SLEEPY SUNBAKED ROSWELL, PAUL'S MOTORCYCLE GAVE UP THE GHOST. WITH ONLY SIXTY BUCKS IN HIS POCKET, PAUL HAD TO STICK AROUND AND EARN ENOUGH MONEY TO GET THE BIKE BACK ON THE ROAD.

THROUGH A RANDOM RECOMMENDATION, AND ON THE STRENGTH OF HAVING A COLLEGE DEGREE, HE SCORED A JOB WRITING POLICE REPORTS FOR THE LOCAL PAPER. ALMOST IMMEDIATELY HE DISCOVERED BOTH HIS SKILL FOR WRITING AND HIS JOY IN THE PROCESS. SUDDENLY, HE WAS A JOURNALIST. AND HE LOVED IT. THAT LOVE, AND THE WORK HE BECAME IMMERSED IN, CARRIED HIM AROUND THE GLOBE. ROSWELL WAS WHERE PAUL DISCOVERED HIS OPEN ROAD.

"I GOT TO WHERE I AM BY NO SORT OF PREPLOTTED LINE," PAUL TOLD US. "NO CAREER-ORIENTED, WELL-THOUGHT-OUT PLAN. I WAS GOING WHERE THE STORY WAS.

"IT'S EASY TO SAY 'FIND YOUR PASSION,' BUT PEOPLE DON'T APPRECIATE AS MUCH THE POWER OF SERENDIPITY IN THEIR LIVES. I HEAR A LOT ABOUT THE WORD PASSION. IT'S A POPULAR WORD THESE DAYS, ESPECIALLY IN THE UNITED STATES. I THINK IT'S OVERUSED. IT'S BEEN DEVALUED. IT'S LIKE A COIN THAT'S BEEN RUBBED TOO MUCH. BUT WHAT ABOUT WHEN SOMETHING HAPPENS AND IT KNOCKS YOU OFF-KILTER; WHAT'S YOUR REACTION? IT MIGHT BE IRRITATION, OR FRUSTRATION, BUT WHEN YOU LOOK BACK ON IT TEN YEARS FROM NOW YOU MIGHT SAY, 'I'M REALLY GLAD THAT HAPPENED BECAUSE I'VE ACCUMULATED THIS SINCE THEN.' SO, YOU HAVE TO BE OPEN TO THESE 'YS' IN YOUR ROAD, AND OPEN TO BEING MOVED BY NEW EXPERIENCES."

STRAIGHT LINES VERSUS TANGENTS. CREDENTIALS VERSUS EXPERIENCES. FALLBACKS VERSUS WHIMS. PLANNING VERSUS SERENDIPITY. IN THE COURSE OF TWO DAYS IN THE DESERT, WE'D MET TWO SUCCESSFUL PEOPLE WHO COULDN'T HAVE HAD MORE CONTRASTING WORLDVIEWS AND STARKLY DIFFERENT LESSONS TO SHARE WITH US. WERE THEY BOTH RIGHT? COULD ONE BE WRONG?

AFTER LEAVING PAUL, I SPENT THE REST OF THE DAY DEBATING IN MY HEAD. THE ADVICE OF EACH OF THEM HAD SEEMED BULLET-PROOF IN THE MOMENT. AND THEY HAD BOTH LED THE LIVES TO BACK UP EVERY ONE OF THEIR WORDS. YET THEY WERE SUCH CONTRADICTIONS!

WE PULLED INTO WHITE SANDS NATIONAL MONUMENT. HAPPY TO BE FREE OF THE RV AND OUR ROUND-ROBIN DISCUSSION, WE SPRINTED OUT INTO THE VAST VOID OF THE EVENING DESERT. ONCE WE WERE ATOP THE DUNES, ANKLE-DEEP IN SAND, THE TRUE LESSON OF THESE TWO CONTRASTING STORIES BECAME CLEAR.

WE SHOULDN'T MODEL OUR LIVES AFTER ANYONE ELSE'S. NEITHER IS RIGHT, AND NEITHER IS WRONG. TO BLINDLY FOLLOW AN EXAMPLE, NO MATTER HOW WELL-CONCEIVED, PUTS US RIGHT BACK ON THE ASSEMBLY LINE. DEON AND PAUL EACH DISCOVERED A SET OF VALUES TO GUIDE THEIR DECISIONS, AND SO MUST WE. EACH ONE OF US ON OUR OWN OPEN ROAD.

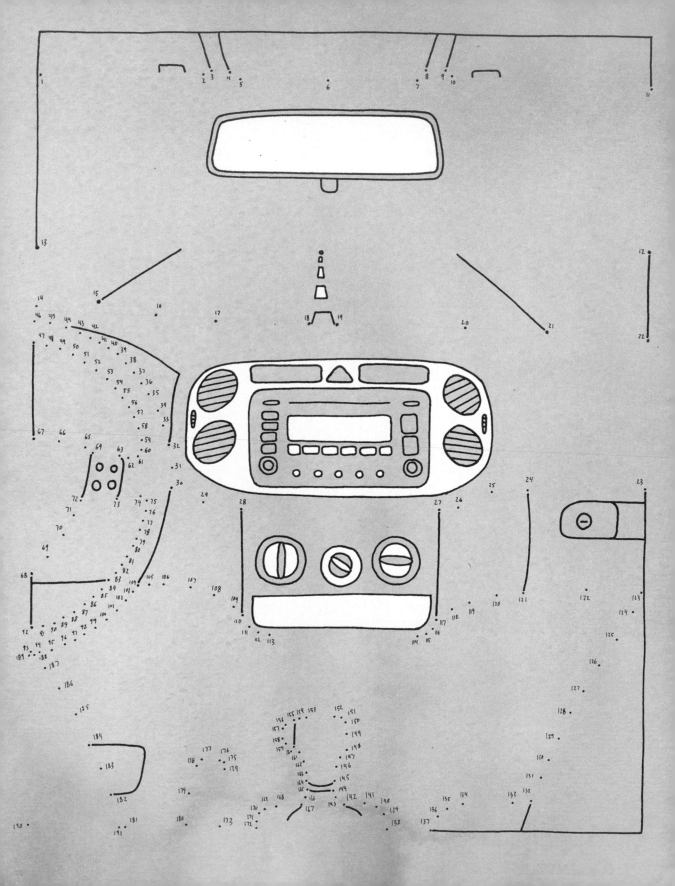

CHAPTER 4

LIFE IS LINEAR ONLY IN THE REARVIEW MIRROR

What do Joe Quesada, editor-in-chief of Marvel Comics; Howard Schultz, chairman of Starbucks; Beth McCarthy-Miller, a director on *Saturday Night Live*; and J. Craig Venter, the scientist who decoded the human genome, have in common?

For starters, their enormous successes might boggle your stressed-out mind, making you feel like you should just give up now and binge out on doughnut holes and reality TV. Shake it off! The stories of these Leaders should actually shine some light on your own "What am I doing with my life?" conundrum. What these successful people share with each other is something we've almost all faced at some point: They too had no idea what they wanted or what they were doing with their lives.

Howard Schultz did not wake up one day in his youth and decide that the world needed to be ordering grande sugar-free, upside-down caramel coffee drinks at a place called Starbucks. When J. Craig Venter was caring for amputees and men with head wounds in Vietnam as a combat medic, he was worlds away from making one of the greatest scientific breakthroughs of all time. Beth McCarthy-Miller didn't have her own instant epiphany, either. When she was folding and shelving cable-knit sweaters at Gap just so she could afford

Christmas presents, she didn't have a concrete vision of directing Tina Fey and Jimmy Fallon at the Weekend Update desk on *Saturday Night Live*, or coaching Will Ferrell on how to ask for "more cowbell."

It's easy to assume that role models had some kind of genius master plan, a straight and secure path that led them to the top. In a haze of fear about our own choices, we assume successful people didn't face our same fears or ever take a step that led them astray. But they did. Often.

If the successful people we've met did not have a clear sense of where they were going before they got there, how *did* they get where they are today? Through years of missteps, failures, epiphanies, and course corrections. Their "direction" was more of a compass heading. A loosely guided approach informed by intention and interest (and plenty of hard work), not by some heavily plotted game plan.

"I had no clue what I was going to be, or what I even wanted to be, when I was in high school," Terry Lickona, the producer of *Austin City Limits* told us. Or what about Jim Koch? Thanks to ever-present football season beer commercials, he's the widely recognized founder and brewmaster of Samuel Adams. When asked about his starting point, he told us, "I was twenty-four years old, and it dawned on me that I was going to need to make career decisions soon, and I felt totally unprepared to do that, because I'd never done anything but go to school my whole life. So I actually dropped out of school. I decided to use my twenties for what they're best for, which is screw around and try lots of things."

It's in the trying that things start to gel.

Life, as Randy Komisar told us, is linear only in the rearview mirror. In the thick of your day-to-day experience, you may feel derailed, but if you're living a life guided by your interests, all those twists and turns, doubts and misfires, will look like a clear path in retrospect.

/ / / Roadmap / / /

DON'T LOOK FOR THE FINISH LINE

"A lot of people I see cannot define what the ultimate goal is," says Randy. "And that paralyzes them because they say, 'Unless I can solve that problem, I can't move forward.' You don't need an ultimate goal. If you are conscious of every day, you will learn every single minute. And if you just follow those steps—looking for your passion and motivation, and doing something that's constructive and supportive of that—ten years from now you can look back and define your path as linear."

It's pretty much impossible at age twenty-one (or at any age) to know what will make you happy for the rest of your life. That's like playing darts blindfolded. The linear goal is an unnatural construct of the Assembly Line mindset. It defies both the way the world works and the way human nature works. The key is to give ourselves the flexibility to make adjustments when we're no longer fulfilled by something. This calls for an elastic approach to life that is adaptable, evolving, and builds on itself—because who wants to stay trapped in a situation they've outgrown, or don't even want, just because they've already "made it this far?"

This mindset of adaptability doesn't mean you should throw caution to the wind and cease all life planning. While we've found that the happiest people didn't follow a fixed formula, what they did follow was their interests and values, and aligned their decisions accordingly. Instead of clinging to rigid, premeditated ideas of where they would end up, they let their paths be informed by experience, which allowed them to respond to new epiphanies and alter their courses when it was necessary.

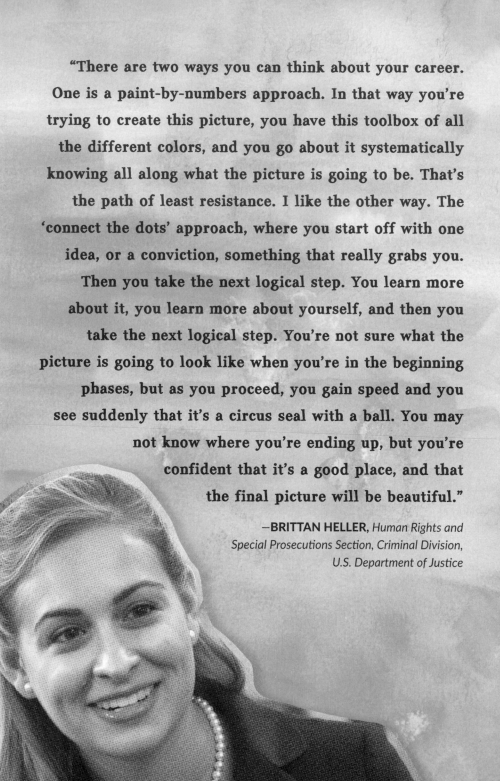

"There are two ways you can think about your career. One is a paint-by-numbers approach. In that way you're trying to create this picture, you have this toolbox of all the different colors, and you go about it systematically knowing all along what the picture is going to be. That's the path of least resistance. I like the other way. The 'connect the dots' approach, where you start off with one idea, or a conviction, something that really grabs you. Then you take the next logical step. You learn more about it, you learn more about yourself, and then you take the next logical step. You're not sure what the picture is going to look like when you're in the beginning phases, but as you proceed, you gain speed and you see suddenly that it's a circus seal with a ball. You may not know where you're ending up, but you're confident that it's a good place, and that the final picture will be beautiful."

—**BRITTAN HELLER,** *Human Rights and Special Prosecutions Section, Criminal Division, U.S. Department of Justice*

The thing about this approach to life is, it won't make sense in the moment. We know the uncertainty is unnerving, and right about now, you're probably thinking, "But can't I just go to law/medical/business/whatever school and wake up a happy, well-adjusted grown-up who owns nice things?" Well, sure you can. Just know that whatever grown-up future you try to orchestrate can change dramatically with time and experience.

Vicki Smith,* a designer at the video game company Vicarious Visions, stresses the importance of diving in first and then evaluating your happiness and satisfaction along the way. Vicki began with a dream of drawing comic books for a living. "It wasn't my parents' dream that their daughter would become a comic-book artist and writer. As much as they loved me and encouraged me, they said, 'We're not going to pay for a humanities degree.' So I went and got my degree in electrical engineering. It's a really good career. But I had that creative side, and essentially I got really bored."

Vicki eventually quit her engineering job and tried a bunch of other paths. She traveled to West Africa and taught for a few years, and later became a teacher in the States. After a few years of trial and error, her path looped back toward the creative realm. "I got my master's in interactive technology. Which is a euphemism for a master's in video game design." How close is Vicki's current career to her original dream of making comic books? Surprisingly close, as she explains: "So I get to make three-dimensional, interactive comic books now. I get to build a castle and figure it out. It's my story. It's my level. So I'm not actually in comic books, but I kind of got a step up."

* **www.roadtripnation.com/leader/vicki-smith**

Starting with comics, Vicki ended up in video games, with a stopover in Africa. She approached her interests from another angle, surprising herself and those around her. Sounds kind of like improv, right? (Which gives us a perfect segue. . . .)

GET FLEXIBLE

Charna Halpern,* founder of ImprovOlympic (now iO) in Chicago, Illinois, is a prime example of intentional but unpredictable living. Charna's path was, at first, clear to her. She was a schoolteacher, and along the way convinced herself that that's exactly who she was. But then a chance radio interview in her hometown led to a job offer to become a radio host.

"I said, 'I don't know anything about being on the radio, I'm a schoolteacher.' But then I started thinking, 'Who said I have to be a teacher? Maybe I am a radio broadcaster!'" That spirit of grasping unexpected opportunities outside of her comfort zone led Charna to work with the influential comedy troupe The Second City and, eventually, to launching her own improv company where she trained comedic legends like Mike Myers and Chris Farley.

* ▶ **www.roadtripnation.com/leader/charna-halpern**

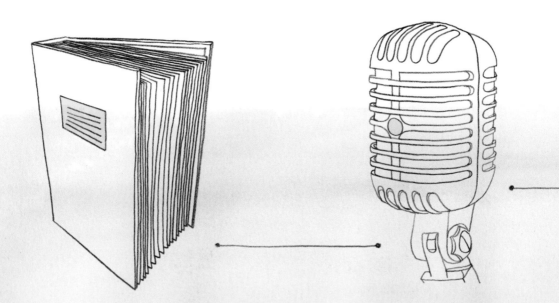

Flexibility is key. Just ask any biologist: Which species survive in the face of change? The adaptable ones. So be nimble and intentional with your choices. Don't think that you have to know the future. Charna's Noise was telling her to believe in only one vision of herself. Instead, she defied those expectations and stayed malleable, finding new ways to define herself. The unexpected twists and turns she followed in life put her on a path that, while you'd never recommend as a strategy, makes total sense in hindsight. As Charna explained it, **"Life is a lot like improvisation. What happens is more interesting than what you've planned, what you planned will never happen, and if you think you know what's going to happen, you're doing it wrong."**

CHAPTER 5
LIVING IN BETA

People will tell you to choose a path and stick to it—stay on course—look for a secure career container and hold onto it like it's a life preserver and you're on the *Titanic*. But they're ignoring the reality of how the world works—and the reality of how you can navigate it in a unique, personal way and thrive like never before.

The "career" as we once knew it is extinct. Not only have economic models changed, but the pace of innovation and diversification continues to accelerate. "You have no idea what field you'll be working in ten to fifteen years from now, because most of those fields don't exist yet," says Juan Enriquez,* an author and researcher who studies the intersection of science, economics, and society. Juan's personal story bears out the truth of his statement. He started out as an official in the Mexican government, and after a stint as a peace negotiator during Mexico's Zapatista rebellion, Juan got tired of getting shot at and went back to academia. He studied genomics, learning about recombinant DNA and other life sciences that to outsiders may seem like straight-up sci-fi. The more he got involved in his field, the more he started to believe that many of the cutting-edge discoveries in genomics could be applied to benefit international economies.

Synthesizing science, business, and sociology, his path led him to found Biotechonomy, a life sciences research and investment firm that focuses on innovative start-ups and companies. Juan didn't wait for this hybridized "career"

  www.roadtripnation.com/leader/juan-enriquez

to show up in some occupational handbook from the Department of Labor, he went out and invented it. Just because something didn't exist twenty years ago, or even ten days ago, doesn't mean it can't exist now.

You, your relationships, the economy, and technology are ever-evolving. So it doesn't make sense to approach life and work like they're cast-iron constants. To deftly navigate the future and be able to grow and thrive amid the challenges, we have to flex our muscle for tolerating uncertainty. This isn't so much a warning as it is an invitation to approach life the way so many of the Leaders we spoke with have already been doing for years: Live in Beta.

LOOK FOR THE NEXT YOU

You've probably heard of (or been part of) a beta test. The beta version of software is typically a limited release in order to test the effectiveness of the product, and its content and format will evolve as the developers discard what doesn't work about it and strengthen what does. A beta test is an iteration of something that is subject to continued improvement.

This approach matches the way we as people should change over time. Living in Beta means you are continually building better versions of yourself. It means that the current "you" is just a single iteration of what you can be, and the next "you" that you build isn't a final either—it's just one more step forward.

No one else we've met demonstrates the ability to iterate and make adjustments quite like Mark Inglis.* Mark, a professional mountaineer who began climbing when he was twelve years old, told us that in his field, "you have to be prepared to be scared on a regular basis, and I guess that set me up incredibly well for all the changes that have happened in my life."

  www.roadtripnation.com/leader/mark-inglis

Mark lost both legs below the knee to frostbite on Christmas Eve, 1982, during an ill-fated expedition up Mount Cook, New Zealand's highest peak. When we sat across from him twenty-six years later, the wind outside howling through the black New Zealand night, he told us:

> "The one thing I've come to understand is [that] the most exciting thing about life is change."

All we could think was, damn . . . this guy had survived some of the most difficult challenges someone could face and was still urging us to embrace the fear and uncertainty that comes with change. When discussing life after the accident, Mark remembers after the surgery looking down at where his legs had been and thinking, "How can I turn this into an advantage?" He told us that his tragedy became a way to re-form people's ideas about disabled people. Change for him meant accepting losing his legs and framing his accident not as a tragedy, but as an opportunity to take advantage of a new landscape. So dogged was he in his desire to prove to the world that he had no limitations that he went on to win a silver medal in the 2000 Paralympic Games and become the first double amputee to summit Mount Everest.

Don't dismiss Mark's story as too extreme for all of us facing less intense challenges. No matter what obstacles we must overcome, our lives will always be in a state of flux. You'll have to roll with unforeseen challenges such as getting laid off, moving to a new place, dealing with death and loss, overcoming personal demons, and even developing a new skill that feels beyond you. These are all moments where you operate in a new version of your life. They are moments where you define who you're going to be, when you push forward into new experiential territory to build a better version of yourself.

AVOID CERTAINTY

It's difficult to accept, but possibility actually exists *within* ambiguity and confusion. As Jad Abumrad,* the host of WNYC's award-winning program *Radiolab*, says, "Premature certainty is the enemy."

"I went to school for music composition," says Jad. "And I was pretty sure that I was going to be a musician. Specifically, writing music for films. That didn't really work out. I mean, I just wasn't very good at it. And so at a certain point I just kind of gave it up. You know, I'm clearly not a good musician. I'm not a good film scorer. That was what I was thinking at that time. And so I thought I had failed. I thought that my plan was wrong."

* **www.roadtripnation.com/leader/jad-abumrad**

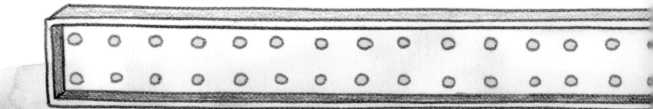

Looking back, Jad remembers the frustration of losing what he thought would be his central force in life. But his girlfriend (and future wife) helped push him to take a different perspective on his setback.

"She said, 'You kind of like to write. You kind of like to make music. You're not really good at either on their own terms, but maybe you could somehow find the middle ground. Try out radio.' So I went and I volunteered for a year making no money, working odd jobs when I could to sort of support myself. It somehow turned out to be more interesting than I expected. It was like this little arrow that pointed me in a direction."

"Composer Jad" was an earlier, not-quite-right iteration of the person Jad was capable of becoming. So the next version of Jad was born. The uncertainty of his future and the concessions he had to make certainly wore on him—but the undeniable satisfaction he got out of the job couldn't be ignored. Following those arrows led Jad to create and cohost *Radiolab*, a show that combines storytelling, philosophy, and science in a sonic way.

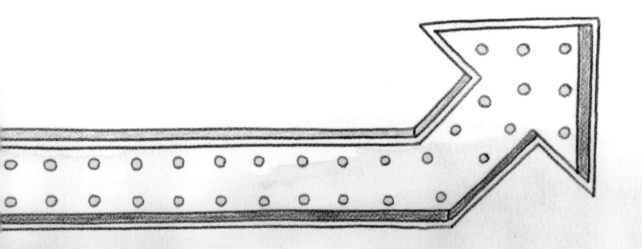

Living in Beta helped push Jad to the next iteration. "I sort of see it as like your future self is leading you in some sense. It's dropping little hints. I would never have known that this is actually the job I was imagining. I didn't have the skills to imagine forward far enough."

Living in the uncertainty of beta is never a cakewalk. Especially when it's 2:00 A.M., we're jittery with anxiety, and we log on to Facebook only to be slapped in the face by a barrage of boasts from our friends.

Date night!! #blessed

Anyone got good tips for cool places to eat in Tokyo? My job is sending me there for two months. STOKED

Cocktails and sunset on the roof deck! I <3 Maui!!!

First of all, step away from the smartphone and unclench your fists. Despite what those carefully curated images on Instagram seem to imply, even these self-congratulating friends have no safe and secure plan for where life will take them. Adapting to the next "you" is an exercise in fear, risk, and bravery.

This act of Self-Construction is difficult, and it happens over and over, in every iteration of your life. Living in Beta doesn't mean you're freaking out that your company might downsize and you'll be out of a job; it means knowing that if your company downsizes and you're out of a job, you'll be okay because of the hard work you've been doing strengthening who you are and what you're good at, rather than blindly holding onto a "career."

Conversely, you can work the same job for forty years and also Live in Beta.

Living in Beta applies universally, because we are all subject to the disruptions that come from change. Even if you're a doctor and you want to stay in the same job for your entire life, you still need to evolve and embrace the changes and advances in your field. Adopting the Living in Beta approach allows us to ride the changing tides, acquire new skills, be open to new experiences, try things out, and let go of the idea that who we are now is all we'll ever be.

So how do you build new iterations of yourself? What are some simple ways to Live in Beta whether you're twenty-two and starting out on the road, or forty-seven and deep into a career you don't like, or fifty-six and happy with where you're at? How do you keep constructing who you are? One answer: To Live in Beta, you have to crave the tension that comes from being on the razor's edge.

Jad encouraged us to reframe discomfort and fear. He advocated a 180-degree shift, wherein feelings of dread, anxiety, and inadequacy are signposts we must *run at* to push our ever-expanding borders. He told us, "You might be at the margins of something great. And things always get tense at the margins. It's like the physics of a liquid changing to a gas: The molecules start to vibrate, and they get very agitated, and then they change to a gas. So things are never happy at the moment of change. Things are always unhappy. And sometimes that unhappiness just means that you're doing something worth doing."

It is in this place of discomfort that we evolve into a new beta self we didn't know was within us. We thrive on a project we thought we'd botch. We get up the nerve to be honest with someone in a way that scares us. We watch ourselves cope with stress we thought would crush us. We come up with a brilliant idea in the eleventh hour. All of these moments help us break into a new, stronger version of ourselves. When a Roadtripper asked Jad how to know when it's time to change, he responded, "You should be panicking a certain percentage of the time, because then you're right at the edge of what you can do. You need a little bit of 'uh-oh' in your life. Just enough."

Radiolab has earned a loyal following as well as a Peabody Award for broadcast excellence in public radio—and its podcast has pushed it to ever-new audiences, young and old. Despite this success, Jad told us he's constantly searching for new ways to shake up the formula of the show. This has meant developing a live show experience and taking it on the road, as well as opening up his ProTools sessions for listeners to remix the show.

Instead of shriveling up on the vine, we have to engineer those uh-oh moments that shake up our lives. It is only in creating beta version upon beta version that we construct a life that's surprising, fulfilling, and ultimately better than we thought possible.

"At *Radiolab*, we're trying anything and everything we can think of to shock us out of our comfort zone, because that's going to lead you to the next version of yourself. Who you are next year and the year after that, that's unknown. I want to get to that person, and I want to be surprised when I meet him. I don't want to just look into the future and see the person I thought I was going to be. That's the worst thing in the world. I just want to be surprised by who I become."

—**JAD ABUMRAD**, *host of WNYC's award-winning program* Radiolab

CHAPTER 6
WHAT IS SUCCESS?

- -

What is success? It's different for everybody. Simple as that. The real question is one we can't answer: What is success to you? Not to your parents, your boss, or your followers on Instagram. What is it to *you*?

We live in a society obsessed with outward displays of success. In the dominant worldview, success is a result that's measured mostly by our ability to get things. If you have this and this and this, if you wear these types of clothes, if you make this amount of money, if you live in this neighborhood, if you're married by the time you're this age, if you have 2.5 kids, if you vacation at this resort, you are successful.

The perception of success as a one-size-fits-all destination is—to borrow a phrase from the lovably cephalopodic Admiral Ackbar—"a trap!" The chief fallacy of success is the presumption that we all agree on what it is. And even the most savvy of us can fall for this lie. It's easy to see why. Who doesn't enjoy nice clothes or a slick car? Who doesn't want to humbly brag about their important job or big paycheck? These are basic impulses; it's the reason good advertising can be so devilishly successful at manipulating us. They're not selling us goods we *don't* want to buy. So even when you see through the Noise that surrounds the society-driven idea of "success," it can be incredibly difficult to figure out how to redefine it for yourself.

Doing some heavy lifting on the subject of success is the only way to even start to get a grip on personal satisfaction. When we're on the road for Roadtrip Nation, we are continually rolling our RV from one person's unique little niche in the world to another's. From living rooms to offices, from laboratories to farms, from studios to coffee shops, it requires a certain discipline to help keep the multitude of individuals we encounter from blurring into an indistinct crowd. One technique we've developed is to ask a few standard questions of almost everyone we meet. It's our barometer for gauging some of the big, hard-to-handle ideas we encounter. And there's no other question that gives us such a wide range of answers as "What is success to you?"

"Success is elusive.
Look within."

—*Rodney Mullen, professional skateboarder and entrepreneur*

"My whole life I wanted to be on a sitcom. I just thought being on TV was it. And when I got [cast for] *Arrested Development*, I remember it was so fantastic and it was so fun, but it didn't satisfy the way I thought it was going to. And what it taught me is there's always that thing in life that everybody thinks, 'If I have that, then I'm going to be done.' I think it's really important to practice contentment and enjoying where you're at, because if you don't practice that now, then when you get where you think you want to be, you're still not going to be content."

—TONY HALE, *actor (and Buster Bluth on Arrested Development)*

SUCCESS: WINNING OR LIVING?

Consider the rightly legendary pro skateboarder Rodney Mullen.* Rightly legendary? Let's rephrase that. The man is basically both the Buddha and the Albert Einstein of the skating world. Even if you didn't grow up skating and couldn't care less about the countless tricks he invented, or that in eleven years he won thirty-five out of the thirty-six contests he entered, the fact remains that the image in your mind of what skaters do exists because of Rodney. In his heyday, he was truly unbeatable. But in the midst of that amazing run, he wasn't happy.

"Having a career in skateboarding almost robbed me of the joy I have in skateboarding," remembers Rodney. "It was slavery." The Rodney Mullen storyline of unending success that every fan followed in the skating mags was in fact a sort of prison for the man on the board winning those competitions.

"I defended that title. They call it a 'title.' It's so corny. . . . All those years, I only lost one contest in eleven years. All that did was make me crazy. . . . My dad made me stop. . . . What am I without contests? To be number one, is that important? No, it's not important. Because I just skate."

Rodney's true vision for success developed outside of the competitive arena. After retiring from the pro circuit, Rodney became an innovator in skateboard component design, especially at the company he cofounded in 2002, Almost Skateboards. Through trial and error, luck and patience, and deep personal reflection, Rodney realigned his talents, keeping them on course with what he loves. These days, Rodney's success is guided by asking the question "Do I see a way to manifest not only what I'm good at, but also what I love? Because hopefully they won't be opposed to one another."

  www.roadtripnation.com/leader/rodney-mullen

So what was his answer when we asked him how he defines success?

"Peace," Rodney says. "It's just peace."

On the opposite side of the world from Rodney (and on the opposite side of the success definition spectrum) we met seven-time world champion surfer Layne Beachley.* As a child, she had a goal and focused on it unwaveringly. Layne recalls: "When I was eight years old, I decided I was going to be the best in the world at something." She began competing in every sport she could, but found surfing to be her common denominator; in it she found both success and joy.

Layne became the only surfer to win six consecutive world titles. This took an enormous amount of drive and single-minded focus. For Layne, adhering to that kind of ambition "wasn't a sacrifice, it was a commitment." She adds, "Ultimately, to become successful in anything, you have to be relatively selfish."

For Layne, giving up her adolescence—forgoing the chance to spend her free time socializing and watching TV while munching delicious carb-heavy snacks—was worth it, because for her, coming out on top is the pinnacle of living. It's that Rocky-at-the-top-of-the-steps, arms-triumphantly-raised moment that drives her in everything she does. Her vision of success is a complete 180 from Rodney's. Rodney's idea of success would never have worked for Layne, and vice versa.

Now, remove the skateboard and surfboard from all this, and what do you have? Two opposing definitions of success. Maybe neither is right for you, but what they share is that they were wholly self-defined. Layne didn't become a world

  www.roadtripnation.com/leader/layne-beachley

champion because someone told her to; she did it because she, through sheer force of will, wanted to be the best in the world at something, and surfing was what felt right to her. Rodney's view of success was different from the accomplishments that thrilled his fans. His success was inner peace. For him, success came through enjoying the sport for the sake of sport, and changing it from a win-or-lose equation to a lifestyle. No external influence could have told either of them what true success was for them as individuals.

Rodney and Layne are just two examples of the thousands of personal philosophies we've encountered over the years. We're not saying that Rodney or Layne's version of success is a perfect fit for you, how could it be? But if, like them, you craft your own authentic idea of satisfaction, you'll find yourself getting to places that bring new challenges and delights. This approach requires constant vigilance.

For Ashfaq Ishaq, the founder of the International Child Art Foundation, success didn't come from his previous high-toned career at the World Bank, but when he started a non-profit from scratch and left his other projects to devote himself to it full-time. For Jerry Colangelo, the owner of the Arizona Diamondbacks and the Phoenix Suns, a well-placed trade is at the heart of his vision for success. David Neeleman, founder of JetBlue, says that to him success means simply "to matter." What these examples all share isn't philosophy or tactics, but intention and individuality. Success is self-defined.

To envision your own definition of success, begin by letting go of the big picture. If you cast the net too wide, you'll come back with a vague answer like "Success is being happy." But what does that mean, really? Success shifts from person to person and even within yourself as you age and gain experience.

How do you define success?

To help you get started, spend some time reflecting on others' definitions of success (your friends', family's, society's). Then think about how you would define it for yourself. How is your definition similar? How is it different? What do you want in your life that might be different than what others want?

Write, draw, or collage your thoughts. This space is yours to help you create a vision of what success means to you.

OTHERS' VISION OF SUCCESS

MY VISION OF SUCCESS

When you look at your broad vision of success, it might be overwhelming to think about how to turn big goals (such as "I just want to be happy") into actionable steps.

The more specific you are about what's important in your life, the clearer you'll see what success means to you. Success at work is different from success as a father, which is different from success on a volunteer project, which is different from . . . you get the idea.

So start to break down your broad vision of success:

In my family life, success is _____.

    In my friendships, success is _____.

        Success in a relationship is _____.

        Success at work is _____.

        Financial success means _____.

    Success in _____ is _____.

Success in _____ is _____.

Think about the different parts of your life in terms of their contribution to your idea of success. Is there a common thread that connects these different elements? Instead of a generalization like "I just want to be happy," can you sum up your vision of success so that it encompasses all of those smaller parts of your life?

Give it a try:

To me, success is _____

_____

_____

_____

_____

Wherever we fall on the spectrum, our conception of success has to go deeper than the standard vision. Once we define success for ourselves, based on what satisfies and excites us, we can work toward it. It won't come easy, and when it does arrive, it may not look like the cover of *Travel & Leisure* (or then again, it totally might), but what it will be is genuine, authentic, and deeply true to who we are.

CHAPTER 7

THE BLANK CANVAS

Life is not a to-do list. This is a difficult concept to accept when we're slogging through a long string of daily responsibilities. Emails to answer, meetings to attend, family to call, bills to pay, supermarket aisles to aimlessly wander as we debate the difference between nonfat and sugar-free. None of that ever stops, and it never will. And if we're not careful, our life becomes that to-do list. We may be having fun or we may be totally stressed out and miserable, but either way we are immersed in distraction. The Assembly Line, the Noise, skewed ideas about work-life balance, and preconceived notions about your life's path and success keep you distracted from what's underneath, which is . . . you.

If you strip away the misleading urgency of the daily grind and boil off the excess fat of the Noise, you get to the Blank Canvas. The Blank Canvas is a space where you can begin to sketch who you really are: the core truth of you and your potential. It's the fresh start, the tabula rasa. It's the place where we can find what we want to know about ourselves and why we want to know it, and accessing it is actually a lot less cheesy than we just made it sound.

Getting to the Blank Canvas is like that whole "forest for the trees" metaphor: If you're too deep in something (trees) you can't see the big picture (the whole forest). That's what the first Roadtrip did for us—it put some space between us and the everyday; it gave us room to see and ask the questions we normally avoided.

When we sat with Roy Remer* in the main room of the hospice center where he works, he had the calm and considered air of someone who is living his life in full alignment. But it wasn't always that way. When Roy was in his late thirties, he had been working in publishing and doing fairly well on paper, but he fell in love with the work he was doing as a volunteer at Zen Hospice Project. "There was this little voice in the back of my head, reminding me that there was something else I should be dedicating my life to, and it's this," he explains.

As we know, it's easy to simply ignore that little voice in the name of taking care of business. Roy had found his calling—serving as a peaceful, present witness for people who were undergoing their final passage out of this world— but, as he sums it up, "It can be a difficult thing to give up a career and make a shift like that. It was very challenging in my relationship, I had a lot of fears around it. I was used to making a certain income; now I was going to go work for a non-profit?"

For a while, Roy straddled both worlds. His publishing job kept the lights on, but, as he recalls, "The hospice work became what was nourishing me spiritually." Roy explained that he needed to create space from his routine to get to his version of the Blank Canvas. "I started spending a lot of time in the backcountry . . . sitting out there in this open place of 'What am I supposed to be doing?'" The distance he achieved in his time out in the wilderness helped him envision something he hadn't previously imagined but somehow always knew he needed. "I had to say good-bye to Roy who was the publishing rep so that I could fully embody this new way of living my life."

Roy's final advice to us was to mark our thresholds; that is, to recognize and honor the different phases in our lives, and let them go when it's time. That's the headspace of the Blank Canvas: creating room to become who we are now,

  www.roadtripnation.com/leader/roy-remer

/ / / Roadmap / / /

"Our minds can be so busy. At any given moment there can be so much happening, so many distractions, so many stories we're caught up in, so many fixations on what's going on around us, and within us. . . . As human beings we often get stuck in a place; I see it all the time. People are really stuck with this concrete idea of who they are."

—ROY REMER, *volunteer manager, Zen Hospice Project*

not holding on to who we were yesterday or last year. Getting to our Blank Canvas means giving ourselves permission to change.

Roy was an active searcher, which makes his finding of his path look easy (from the outside, anyway). But many of us, depending on how immersed we are in the Noise, can find the road to the Blank Canvas filled with fits and starts.

Christina Heyniger,* for instance, was so deeply immersed in society's vision of success (and maintaining it) that she had to summon all her will and drive in order to break free. It took her years.

She began, like most of us, a bit adrift, conditioned to chase outward symbols of "success." After attending Cornell, she bobbed around the five boroughs, watching her college friends in NYC climb the ladder toward bigger paydays.

"I started working on the weekends at a cheese stand," Christina recalls. "I would bump into people from Cornell, and they'd say, 'What are you doing here?' And I would answer, 'I don't know what I'm doing here. I'm selling cheese—would you like some?'"

Christina listened to the Noise and panicked. She earned a master's degree, an MBA, and a job as a business consultant. She soon embodied society's vision of success.

Cut to eight years later: Christina was still chugging along on the Assembly Line. Successful, but . . . empty. "The biggest problem was not knowing what inspired me," says Christina. **"I knew I was flatlining at my job, but what I realize now is that I had not created space from my routine to think more broadly. I was getting promoted, and I was doing alright, but I wasn't energized."**

  www.roadtripnation.com/leader/christina-heyniger

In Christina's world, there was nowhere to look beyond the din of her life and the expectations she'd created for herself. "When I thought about different jobs I wanted, I was only thinking in terms of the amount of money I was making at that point. It took me a long time to start questioning the whole foundation of that, which was: maybe I don't need to make this much money, and this house and these responsibilities—maybe I don't have to have them! Whoa. Suddenly there were crazy options!

"The real turning point for me was a trip to the Grand Canyon, because [there] I was completely disconnected from everything." Christina had grown up in Alaska, far from the urban playground she'd turned into her home, and there was something about rafting through the Grand Canyon that reawakened old joys she'd since put aside. That distance from the endless routine of work and the seductive trappings of her everyday "success" allowed her to reevaluate and take stock of her life. What truly made her happy? What was she missing, and how could she get it back? This was her Blank Canvas moment. Not long after that, she left New York, became a river guide, and then started using her business skills to help tourism companies. Eventually she founded the New Mexico–based Xola Consulting, which specializes in developing sustainable adventure tourism.

"The thing that everybody has to give is their joy," Christina says. "I define my success by my joy. Even when I'm sad, I'm still so joyful. Joyful! About what I'm doing. I'm so alive, and I feel so creative and generally thrilled. I'm the most successful I could ever imagine being because I'm so stinking happy."

Don't get us wrong, we're not advocating that everyone quit their jobs and become bearded backwoods artisanal soap makers. Getting to the Blank Canvas requires space, but it doesn't have to be the space around a moonlit campfire. It can just be a switch-up, something to rattle you and challenge you.

LET CHANGE HAPPEN

Jamaican-born, Canadian-raised Charline Gipson* quit her corporate law job in New York City not so she could go herd sheep or make abstract art—she simply went to a new city and explored a new avenue of the law.

"So here's the thing," recalls Charline. "I had my job in New York, everything was great, I was making tons of money, but I knew something was wrong; I felt it was unfulfilling. I literally said to myself one day: 'So, am I just supposed to buy stuff until I die? Just collect more junk?' But I was so busy—I was billing so many hours—I felt like I was on a treadmill and I didn't have the emergency pull-it-to-stop. So I accepted a job in New Orleans to be a law clerk for a federal court judge."

With this decision, Charline dropped a few rungs on the lawyer status ladder, but she knew she had to do it. "It was kind of my way to still be supporting myself, but step off the treadmill, and then have all this free time to figure out what the hell is wrong with me." That free time—that immersive change—helped her realign her vision, which ultimately led to Charline opening her own firm with a colleague in New Orleans. Charline admits that it can be scary to make these kinds of changes. But it's a good kind of scary. "It feels like you're stepping off of a cliff, and it doesn't make any sense, and it's irrational, but that's when you're most alive." And change, of course, is life's only constant. In a way, envisioning your Blank Canvas is a tool to take control of the inevitability of change.

  www.roadtripnation.com/leader/charline-wright-gipson

Roy, the Zen Hospice volunteer director, calls this process dress-rehearsing for death. He talked about sitting with the dying, and the fear and regret he witnesses in those last moments. "When I am sitting with someone who is unprepared because they've lived a life so attached to this idea of who they are, and they haven't allowed that idea to really shift in big ways, it can be really, really painful for them."

Essentially, what Roy is warning us about is the fact that we can become so attached to an idea of who we are that we refuse to grow and let the past be gone. We should practice letting go of phases of our lives when we've outgrown them. "It's a radical concept," Roy acknowledges, "but [it helps] to practice dying while you're healthy. This allows us to honor who we've been, make peace with it, and move into who we are now."

That's what this book has been about so far: getting rid of the old notions of yourself to get to something truer.

You've already been priming yourself to let go of all those layers of artifice. Getting to the Blank Canvas isn't like going to the store and picking up a new one. You get only one canvas, and yours may already have a ton of work done on it. Some of it might be great—the real workings of a masterpiece in progress— but other parts may be forced strokes from the Noise and lines from society's paint-by-numbers approach. But we have to work with what we've got, and the only way to get down to that clean slate is to delete all the autofill and busy work. It is time to let go of all the things that aren't you.

What are the things you need to let go of? See if you can fill in a few blanks:

The Noise I used to accept was _____, but now

I know how to shed it.

I used to think success was _____, but now my

own definition of success is _____.

I used to call myself a _____, but that really

has nothing to do with who I really am.

I was a _____, but I no longer am.

When people asked _____, I would tell them

_____ even though I knew it wasn't true.

I was thinking I would be _____, but does this

really reflect what I want for myself?

I was a _____, but I've learned all I can,

and it is time I move on.

We'll admit this kind of transformation can feel difficult, maybe even terrifying. Does wiping the slate clean invalidate all the work you've put in? Are you disappointing your family? Your friends? Yourself? Does this mean you are a complete screw-up if you've gotten as far as you have but it's not where you want to be? Or maybe you feel like everyone around you is pressuring you to stay the same, as if they have a bigger stake in your life than you do.

Whatever those nagging voices are, ignore them. Open yourself to the possibility of new versions of yourself. Reject the idea that you already know what you're capable of. Silence the voices that question your skills and stop you from exploring your untapped talents. Know that beneath your surface are dormant parts of you that have yet to be unearthed.

Now, just look forward. As Roy explained, "Whether it be graduation, a divorce, a death in our life, a change in career, or whatever . . . we're watching each moment as it passes away, and each moment anew as it comes up for us. *This is who I was yesterday. That's gone. This is who I am today.*"

DEF

PART TWO ::::::::::::::::::::::::::::::::

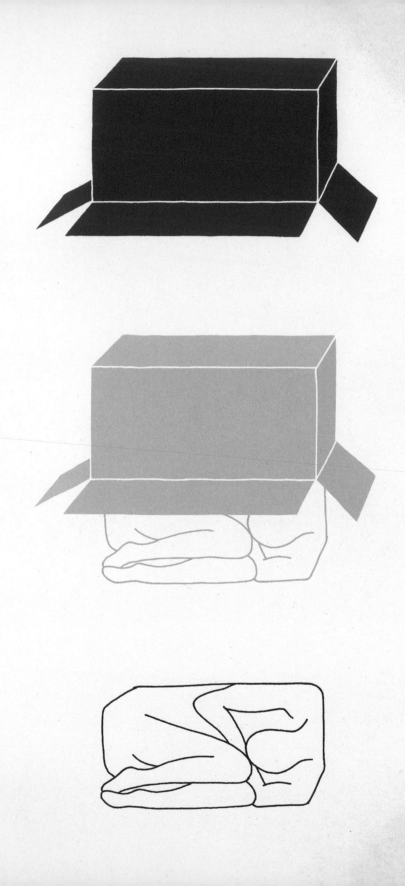

CHAPTER 8

PURSUE YOUR INTERESTS—NOT AN OCCUPATION

A while back, as we sat around the table at Roadtrip Nation HQ, we discussed the many things we'd like this book to communicate. One of the most important took some time to flesh out. Just like in a classic detective novel, the answer had been in front of our faces the whole time. That's just how it goes: The most obvious and undeniable truths are often the most difficult to see. The discovery? **We have to kill the "career."**

Within every conversation we'd had on the road, there was a clear and consistent trend underlying each story, regardless of age, culture, creed, gender, and geography. The people we met did not pursue an occupation—they pursued their interests. The "career" had been dead for a while, and it was time to admit it.

Imagine you only get to wear one shirt, or dress, or smock, or whatever, for the rest of your life. And you have to go to the store right now and pick it out, but you don't get to pick the store, nor do you get to try the item on. You can't check whether it fits right or matches your complexion or is itchy as hell or smells weird. You just take a quick look and decide, and that's what you'll wear forever. That would be ridiculous, of course. Yet this is the absurd method of the old-school paradigm that forces us to squeeze ourselves into a career that's supposed to be forever.

A career is

a container.

A career is a container, nothing more. The traditional career model forces you to pick a career in high school or college and then reverse-engineer yourself into it.

It's like all those by-the-book personality tests that funnel us into an absolute prescription for our future (such as "Based on your responses you'll be best suited to be a nurse"). Maybe there's an essential truth in that statement, but that narrow diagnosis often ignores key parts of our personalities. What if you pass out at the sight of blood? That doesn't mean you can't build a life around helping people, but maybe the emergency room just isn't the place for you. The problem is that the pencil-in-the-bubble tests don't ask you to engage with your results. It's nothing more than an authority-imposed mandate that doesn't speak to who you are or how you interact with the world. The interest-based approach we're proposing is the opposite. It's expansive. Instead of being assigned an *output*, you are able to explore a world of options based on your *input*. Instead of leaving with a narrowed-down version of what you could be, this approach broadens the scope of what's possible for you.

We are each way too dynamic and unique to cram into a one-size-fits-all mold. Choosing a career forces you to make decisions about something when you have limited experience about what that something really is. But those who've climbed out of the career container tend to find exciting, unexpected ways to connect personal satisfaction to financial stability and success. How did they do it? How will you do it?

You start with your interests.

"You have to find something that allows some piece of your soul—the part that you're passionate about—to participate. If you turn your back on that, you're setting yourself up for misery."

—**CHRIS FLINK**, *partner, IDEO*

If you're among the harried readers looking for a distillation of this book (antici-pating the "TL;DR" response), here it is. Our message can be reduced to one sentence: *build a life around your interests*. This is the one lesson we hope you take away from this book. Everything else flows from this basic idea. The people who end up the most fulfilled in life put in the effort to incorporate their interests into their work, creating their own unique Worklife. What excites and engages them becomes the starting point for every decision they make on their roads.

The reason the interest-first approach is so much better is because when we're doing what we love, we're alive (and it really sucks to hate your job). But what if you don't know what you're interested in? Whether we know it or not, we have a tendency to sneak the things we love into overlooked corners of our life—we just have to look from a different vantage point to see them. You might discover that you're already engaged in your interests in some way every day.

"You already know the things inside of you that you feel when something is in harmony or is going right. You know it. I mean, it's what makes you giddy; it makes you feel like you're getting away with something. It makes you feel like you're playing."

—ANTHONY VENEZIALE, *associate artistic director, Back House Productions, New York City*

We all know the feeling Anthony's describing. Sometimes, we're engaged in an activity, and time simply vanishes. We get lost in the doing. It's in those moments we might consider trivial that we can discover our interests. Maybe you're posting videos you've made to YouTube on your day off, or hiking in the woods, or volunteering for a political campaign, or building a Frank Lloyd Wright-style house in Minecraft—whatever it is that speaks to you, therein lies your interests.

Exploring those interests, finding ways to fold them into your work, and letting them guide your choices and commitments is the best way to break free from the career container.

If you're not truly interested in medicine, don't listen to the Noise and convince yourself you are because it's an impressive and lucrative profession. And don't be afraid if the interests you uncover don't seem legitimately serious. Especially in today's fractured and diverse marketplace, there are countless surprising ways to integrate your interests into your work. You can take a love of Saturday morning cartoons all the way to a senior position at the Cartoon Network, as Mike Lazzo did, or you could take a simple fascination with bones all the way to becoming a prominent figure in the world of forensic anthropology, as University of Tennessee Professor Dr. Bill Bass did. The point is, **don't silo yourself.**

Doctors work only in medical offices. Teachers work only in classrooms. All scientists wear lab coats. Programmers only make websites. When we zoom out, it becomes clear that none of those statements are true, but when confronted with trying to forge a new path for ourselves, we can have a failure of imagination in thinking about what it means to work in a certain field or follow a particular interest. The Noise drowns out creative thinking in this moment, confining us. You need to instead question your assumptions and explore to get to the truth.

Take Shawn Lani,* the senior exhibit developer at the Exploratorium museum in San Francisco. At first, Shawn was apprehensive about working in science (despite his love for it), because the stereotype of the scientist, working in a lab all day, didn't appeal to him. He was drawn to that world for other reasons. "There were some things that I loved," Shawn told us. "Like the unknowns. The mysteries. The idea that you can look at a physical object or a place, and there would be more there than you could find. So that interested me, but in such a vague way that it was hard to apply."

Shawn meandered, unable to commit to a particular field. He played piano in a bar and sold shoes. Eventually, he discovered a job that satisfied his love of science and his creative side: creating hands-on museum exhibits in the Exploratorium's playful learning laboratory environment. The whole point of the museum is to encourage curiosity and profound exploration of the physical world, which lets Shawn engage with what he loves about science.

* **www.roadtripnation.com/leader/shawn-lani**

Below are some Core Interests we've identified from meeting with Leaders. Mark the ones that speak to you. We've left a few blank ones for you to fill in if you think of more.

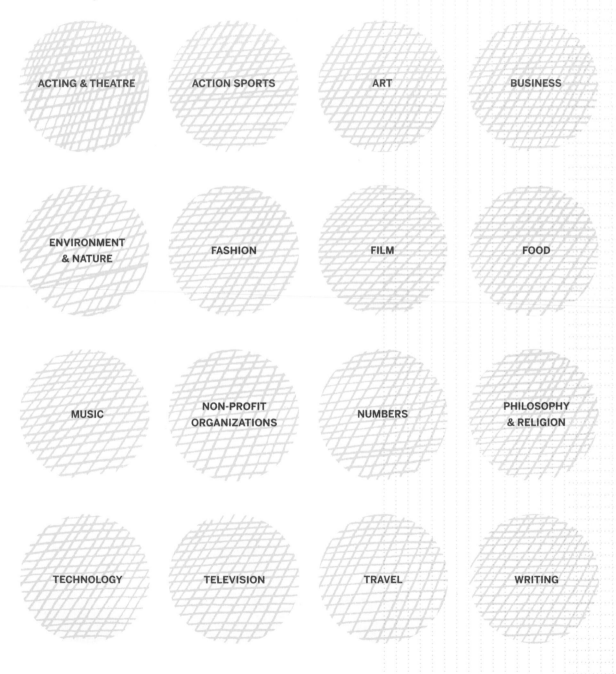

ACTING & THEATRE

ACTION SPORTS

ART

BUSINESS

ENVIRONMENT & NATURE

FASHION

FILM

FOOD

MUSIC

NON-PROFIT ORGANIZATIONS

NUMBERS

PHILOSOPHY & RELIGION

TECHNOLOGY

TELEVISION

TRAVEL

WRITING

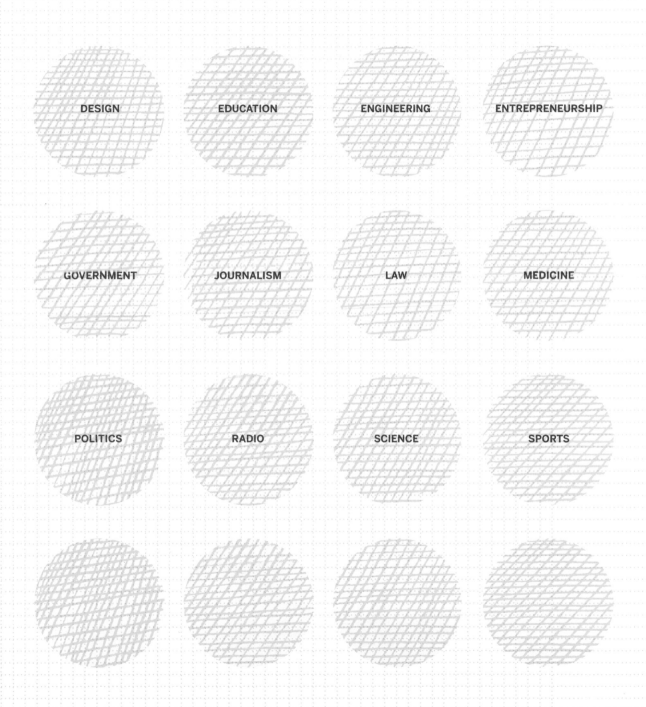

DESIGN

EDUCATION

ENGINEERING

ENTREPRENEURSHIP

GOVERNMENT

JOURNALISM

LAW

MEDICINE

POLITICS

RADIO

SCIENCE

SPORTS

These interests may seem obviously appealing—things that you or just about anyone might be into—but there is actually a lot more to them. To help broaden your perspective of how and in what ways different people built their lives uniquely around their interests, dive into the Roadtrip Nation Interview Archive by going to **www.roadtripnation.com/explore/interests**. Take some time to jot down notes and think about these questions:

Were you surprised by all the different ways people crafted their interests into livelihoods? Can you imagine taking an interest further in your own life?

CREATE YOUR WORKLIFE

Transforming an interest into a Worklife takes imagination and courage. Billy King,* the president of the Philadelphia 76ers, understands that sometimes that means taking leaps, taking risks, and simply trying. Billy began with a simple interest: basketball.

"I just wanted to play pro basketball," he told us. "Once I got to school I realized there's more to life than basketball." Just because he loved the sport didn't mean his only option was to play point guard for an NBA team. After graduating from Duke (and between bartending gigs), Billy did color commentary for ESPN and landed a job as a sports analyst at a local TV station. He explored the surprising variety of interests that surround playing basketball, developing his talents, testing options, and always growing. Starting out thinking he wanted to *play* pro ball, Billy developed a lifestyle where basketball is still part of his life—just in ways he never expected. "There are so many people who get caught up in a career," he reminds us, "and they just do it, and the next thing they know, they're six years into it and they hate it."

  www.roadtripnation.com/leader/billy-king

It's that flexibility, creativity, and willingness to pursue an interest when the road ahead is unclear (and maybe a bit scary) that has helped people like Billy find ways to make a living from their interests.

Once you've begun to think creatively about building your life around your interests, don't become static in your thinking. When you think beyond the ordinary and mash your interests together, you'll have a better chance at fulfillment. When we look at the people we've talked to, they followed their interests, but most of them didn't just integrate one interest into their work and daily lives. They took multiple interests and created a mashed-up Worklife that encompasses all the different parts of who they are.

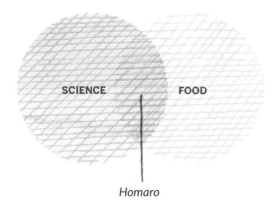

Homaro

No story embodies the power of mixing and matching interests more than that of futurist chef Homaro Cantu.* As a child, Homaro took apart a lawn mower, hoping he'd break it and his dad would stop making him mow the lawn, but in the process discovered he had an affinity for figuring out how things worked. Homaro's love of invention and mechanics eventually intersected with his hardscrabble climb up through the restaurant world (he slept on a couch through culinary school and often worked for free to gain experience on the line). His

 www.roadtripnation.com/leader/homaro-cantu

Chicago restaurant, Moto, is now on the cutting edge of inventive food, pushing the boundaries of molecular gastronomy. From edible menus to "carbonated" fruit, every aspect of Moto's offerings integrates Homaro's love of mechanics with his love of cooking. That is the essence of the mashup: taking two seemingly disparate interests—in this case, food and science—and merging them in unexpected ways through ingenuity and exploration.

The power of the mashup is integral to filmmaker Valerie Weiss's* Worklife. On the one hand, she is a biophysicist with a PhD, but on the other she is a director. "I approach my art as a scientist," she says. "I have a hypothesis, which is that I want to make a movie about something. Then I start collecting data, reading articles, talking to people; I get information. Then I do some experiments—like writing a scene and listening to how it sounds with actors. I'm using these terms loosely, but the scientific method is still the same in how I work on something creative."

The two disciplines informed each other early on when she was a student at Harvard. Although she studied science, she founded a film program at one of the university's student centers. Working in service of her interests, Valerie found that the hard work wasn't a duty, it was a payoff—leading to her directorial film debut in 2003. "When I do what I love, there's no shortage of energy," she told us. "I've had jobs, especially retail jobs, where I had a horrible work ethic because it was depressing and sad to be there. But when I'm doing what I really want to do, I can work around the clock with no rest."

Just as Valerie has experienced, when we look beyond the common examples, we can find connective tissue that brings our interests together. It's that connective tissue that holds the inspiration.

  www.roadtripnation.com/leader/valerie-weiss

SPORTS + JOURNALISM

Ariel Helwani,
MMA SPORTS REPORTER

SCIENCE + ENGINEERING

Brian Binnie,
TEST PILOT FOR SPACESHIPONE

ENTREPRENEURSHIP + TRAVEL

David Neeleman,
FOUNDER OF JETBLUE

FOOD + SCIENCE

Elise Benstein,
FOOD SCIENTIST AT THE
JELLY BELLY CANDY COMPANY

POLITICS + TELEVISION

Jeff Johnson,
POLITICAL ACTIVIST
AND BET HOST

MUSIC + FILM

Lance Bangs,
MUSIC VIDEO DIRECTOR

JOURNALISM + FASHION

Atoosa Rubenstein,
FORMER EDITOR-IN-CHIEF
OF *SEVENTEEN* MAGAZINE

MATH + DESIGN

Rex Gringon,
HEAD OF CHARACTER ANIMATION
AT DREAMWORKS ANIMATION

ART + ENTREPRENEURSHIP

Michelle Dreher,
FOUNDER OF
TWO TONE PRESS

NATURE + GOVERNMENT

Denise Verret,
ASSISTANT DIRECTOR OF
THE LOS ANGELES ZOO

Now take your Core Interests and mash them together. How many different combinations can you think of?

With this new approach, start looking at the world differently. Over the next few days, try to log as many examples as you can of people living lives that combine multiple interests. Look for lawyers in movie credits, engineers working on roller coasters, or accountants working for professional sports teams. The diversity of paths out there is endless and endlessly growing. We're just not taught to look for them.

OCCUPATION   INTEREST   INTEREST

This is how you kill the career and replace it with a Worklife that will be so much more meaningful and sustainable than what came before it. Craft roles for yourself. Invent them when they don't exist. Don't wait to get paid; start doing it, and you'll eventually find a way to get a paycheck for work that embodies your interests. As painter Christopher Brown told us, "Each one of us has never lived before, we're unique people. . . . All you have to figure out is what it is about you that makes you different and make your life a celebration of that thing."

CHAPTER 9

DEFINING YOUR FOUNDATION

Understanding what's truly important to you starts with your interests. They are the building blocks of your identity—the things that engage and excite you. But your interests are only the first component. The more Leaders we speak with, the more we see that there is always *something* tying their interests together. Even if someone's road changed wildly, this something showed up consistently throughout their lives. We've come to call that something a Foundation.

Simply put, your Foundation is the central aspect that reflects what you enjoy doing in the world. It's the underlying reason you're drawn to your interests, and it'll most likely show up in all of them.

Finding that central connection can be the key to finding your road ahead. For example, let's say you love food. That's useful surface-level information you can use as the base of your road. But dig deeper and get to the supporting layers that hold up that interest. What is the fundamental element that draws you to food? Do you enjoy experimenting with recipes and being creative? Do you get satisfaction from working with your hands and raw ingredients? Do you find yourself writing detailed Yelp reviews after every meal? Do you come alive when you teach your niece how to bake cookies? Figuring out what attracts you to your interests can give you greater insight in choosing a road that most aligns with your traits.

Here are some Foundations we've identified in our Leaders throughout the years:

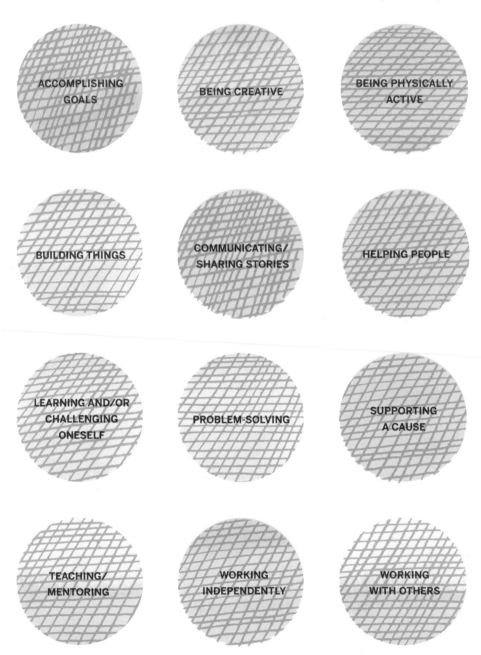

ACCOMPLISHING GOALS

BEING CREATIVE

BEING PHYSICALLY ACTIVE

BUILDING THINGS

COMMUNICATING/ SHARING STORIES

HELPING PEOPLE

LEARNING AND/OR CHALLENGING ONESELF

PROBLEM-SOLVING

SUPPORTING A CAUSE

TEACHING/ MENTORING

WORKING INDEPENDENTLY

WORKING WITH OTHERS

Understanding your Foundation means going beyond the ways in which we normally think about ourselves. This isn't about filling out your online profile or taking a personality test; it's not about your "likes" or character traits. Your Foundation isn't "I'm a nice person," or "I enjoy baking;" it's about the motivation that leads you to such statements. It's "I'm a caregiver" or "I need to be creating something." It is what lights you up at your core. Zeroing in on your Foundation points you toward concrete activities within your interests.

THINK BIG AND THINK BACK

In the case of Richard Meier, the Pritzker Prize–winning architect of the Getty Center, his Foundation is a desire to build things. "When I was growing up," says Richard, "my parents had a basement in their house, and I had a drafting board where I would make drawings and model boats and model airplanes. **I just liked making things.**"

Notice that Richard didn't say that as a kid he "loved architecture." The love of making things brought Richard, very naturally, to architecture, but there were countless other ways he could have manifested that desire, from engineering to carpentry to pottery or rocket science. Like Richard's, your own Foundation doesn't close doors, it simply helps you see which doors you want to open. It will stay with you, supporting you, as you engage in interests that bring it to life.

Think of your Foundation as an unchanging mainstay that will course-correct you in times of confusion. Over time, your interests may change, or your desire to do a certain kind of work may shift, or your financial requirements may grow (or lessen), but your Foundation will most likely stay the same.

133

In fact, our Foundation is probably the same thing that's motivated us ever since childhood, but as we grow up, we tend to ignore the truths we discovered about ourselves when we were younger. The things we didn't place a value judgment on when we were kids suddenly become "impractical," "foolish," or "impossible" as we're urged to grow up and "face reality." So we turn away from the values of our Foundation in favor of a societal stamp of approval and a vision of security.

Such was the case with Washington, DC–based artist Cheryl Foster,* who took twenty years to rediscover her Foundation. Although Cheryl had always had an affinity for the arts, and had done a stint in art school, in the name of security she put away her art supplies and became a real estate appraiser. Cue the long march of years (decades!) on the Assembly Line.

Day by day, a deep sense of resentment and frustration began to consume Cheryl. When we're divorced so deeply from our Foundations, that sense of separation from one's own true identity is gnawing. But no matter how off track we are, we all have the power to reconnect with our Foundation. Simply put, your Foundation is you. Many of us just have to look back, as Cheryl did, and find a memory of what it feels like to be satisfied. "My parents had introduced me to doing things with my hands," recalls Cheryl. "At church, they had hat contests. My mother would create these Josephine Baker–style hats, and

* ▶ **www.roadtripnation.com/leader/cheryl-foster**

we'd win every time!" Resurrecting that source of satisfaction put her on a road that eventually led to a successful and satisfying life immersed in the arts. "This is not a hobby for me; this is me. Turpentine, oil, hot glue guns, that's what's running through my veins!" Though artistic media may have evolved since her childhood, the act of creation was the core principle of Cheryl's Foundation.

Ignoring your Foundation, or not digging deep enough to discover it, is a sure way to amplify your dissatisfactions and frustrations. It might take years to discover, or it might surface tomorrow morning, but as we've seen with so many Leaders, understanding it creates a sense of urgency to act on it.

EXPLORE, DISCOVER, AND DEFINE YOUR FOUNDATION

Start thinking beyond single-slot careers. While you may want to be an engineer, that desire isn't a Foundation. Your Foundation is the underlying characteristic that draws you to engineering. It's the thing that brings meaning to your actions. It's the basic internal impulse that pushes you one way or another. It's what makes you feel fulfilled—not rich, famous, or powerful, but excited, useful, and proud. Go deep and think about what adds substance to all the things you love to do. Remember what consumed your time as a child, or think about what fills your free time now. What is at the core? What is the common thread?

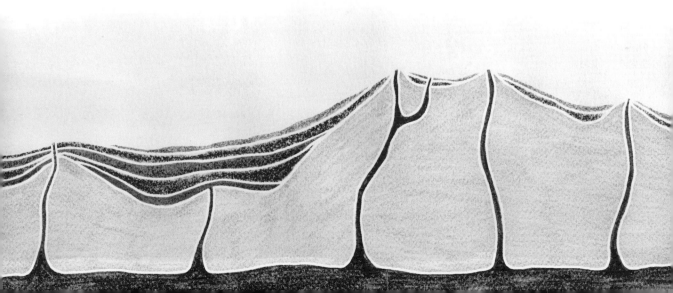

Think of your Foundation as a "need" instead of a "would-like-to."

Try filling in the blank below. For ideas to get you thinking, see the examples that follow and circle those that resonate most.

"As long as I'm _____ I'll be happy."

Working with others/
building relationships

Teaching/mentoring

Building things

Communicating/sharing stories

Helping people

Learning/challenging
myself mentally

Working independently

Upholding a cause I believe in

Being creative

Being physically active

Accomplishing my goals

Problem-solving

Maybe you're still unclear about what your Foundation is. Like we said earlier, self-doubt and confusion can easily follow the Blank Canvas stage. That's okay. To move beyond that, the following questions can help.

WHO ARE YOU NOT?

Sometimes, figuring out who you are is derived from simply identifying who you're not. To get to your Foundation, think about the things that *don't* make up who you are, and what's left will be easier to investigate. There's a nuance here. We don't mean things you like or don't like, but more deeply, things that just don't jive with your identity. Try on each one of these Foundations as if you're in a fitting room. Which ones don't feel right? Which ones could you never imagine engaging you? Start discarding all the things you're not by crossing them off the list.

WHAT IS PLAY TO YOU?

Dreams begin on the playground. "For me, it really starts with this ball," says Kevin Carroll, the author of *Rules of the Red Rubber Ball*. "What is that thing that brings you joy?" Kevin asked us. Often it's in play, whether in our childhood or adulthood, that we find deep and abiding joy. In those moments we can get a glimpse of our Foundation without even knowing it. Examine your play: Where do you lose track of time? What engrossed you in your earlier years that you might be ignoring?

It might not jump out at you immediately, but if you look at the commonalities among the things that excite you, you'll get a window into your Foundation.

Keep thinking broadly about your Foundation and what gives you joy, satisfaction, and a sense of purpose. Refine your own idea of what it means. It might take you a few attempts to find the right Foundation, but that's okay. You'll get there if you're observant.

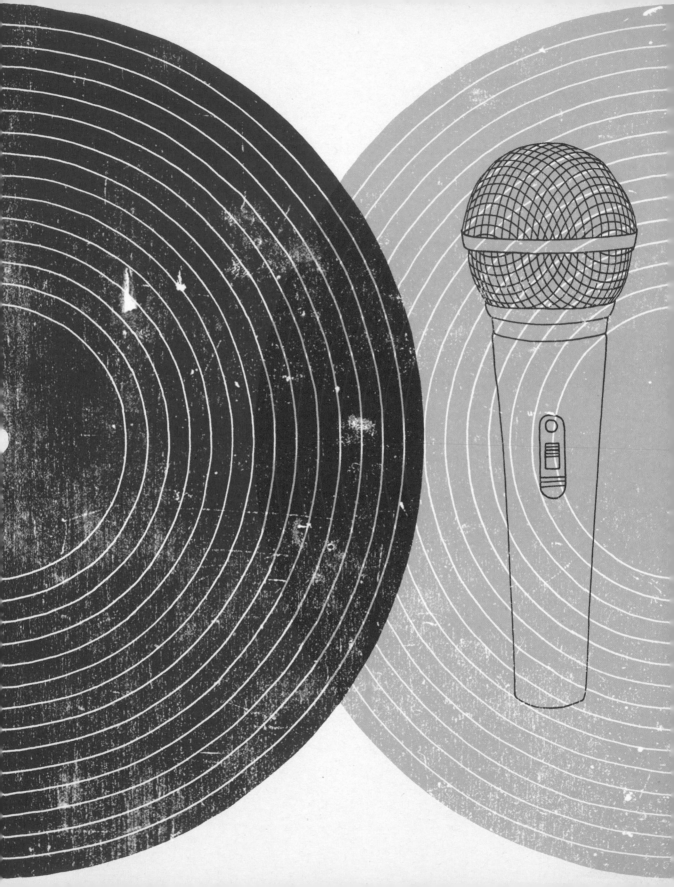

CHAPTER 10

TWO TURNTABLES AND A MICROPHONE

In 1985, the electro-hip-hop act Mantronix released *Mantronix: The Album*. Featuring such iconic dance anthems as "Bassline," "Needle to the Groove," and "Fresh Is the Word," it became one of the most influential albums of the early hip-hop era and, eventually, one of the albums most heavily remixed and sampled by other artists, including the Beastie Boys and Master P.

A decade later, a particularly catchy snippet of "Needle to the Groove" was sampled by Beck in his hit song "Where It's At." The sample is a sort of rallying cry for DJs everywhere: "I got two turntables and a microphone!" We think that's a good call to action, and, as we're about to illustrate, not just for the dance floor.

The DJ, up in the booth, mic in hand, doesn't work from a single record. It's when you combine sounds together that things get interesting. And we can't think of a better metaphor for how to define your own road than this one. In this metaphor, you're the DJ of your life, mixing, merging, and layering the things you care about on top of one another to fashion your own one-of-a-kind record of life.

WHERE IT'S AT

First, you need a carefully built collection of albums, acquired with love and care and countless hours rifling through bargain bins at record shops and thrift stores. These go-to albums, packed with songs and beats you love, are your Core Interests. You start mixing them up, dropping the needle down on old favorites, trying out new tracks, and now you step up to the mic, shouting out a call-and-response to get the crowd going. Consider that mic your Foundation. Interests plus Foundation, working together. The combination of all these elements, when mixed right, creates a balanced, dynamic representation of your life—a seamless synergy of who you are coupled with what you love. Part of Self-Construction is blending together all the things that make you *you*—your Foundation and Core Interests—in effect, creating a blueprint for what you want to do with your life.

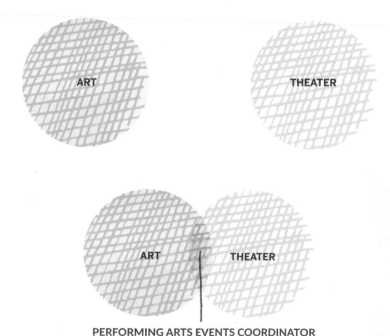

PERFORMING ARTS EVENTS COORDINATOR

"I never knew a job like what I have now existed, or could exist. Your path is what you make of it. You have to just trust that you have something unique to offer."

—**ANA HORTILLOSA**, *Events Coordinator, Asian Art Museum, San Francisco*

THE OPEN ROAD

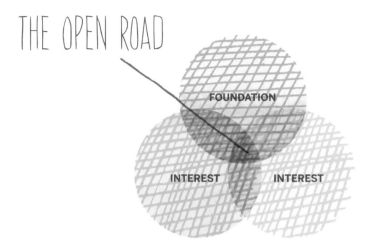

So it's time to create your own unique-to-you masterpiece. It's in the overlap that your Core Interests and your Foundation begin to find their rhythm. You can always mix in new Core Interests to create an endlessly evolving anthem of your own that will see you through all the challenge and change in the years ahead.

Philosophy, anthropology, art, and theater. These are the areas Ana Hortillosa* explored while an undergrad at UC Berkeley. Any one of those four prongs represents the kind of interest that instantly elicits that parental head-shaking, "You'll never get a job" response. Ana felt that pressure. "I wanted to get a 'real' job, but I wanted it to feel right," she told us. Mash those Core Interests up, along with Ana's underlying Foundation—sharing stories—and what did she get? Ana became an event coordinator at the Asian Art Museum in San Francisco. It's not a miracle that she found a job wherein each of her interests, skills, and underlying desires is satisfied. She simply followed her interests, layering them and adapting her Worklife vision as she explored the possibilities.

  www.roadtripnation.com/leader/ana-hortillosa

What's wild about all this mixology, what continually amazes us, is the unexpected quality of it all. Like Ana, many others we have interviewed had no idea where following their Open Road would lead them. But in following it, they arrived somewhere deeply satisfying. Here are just a few of the interesting, diverse places that following your Core Interests and Foundation can lead you to.

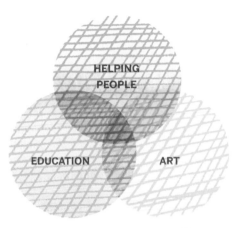

Aleks Zavaleta, **NON-PROFIT DIRECTOR**

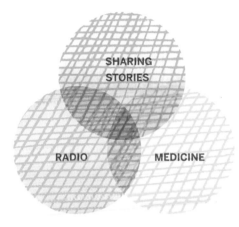

Karl Kruszelnicki, **RADIO HOST**

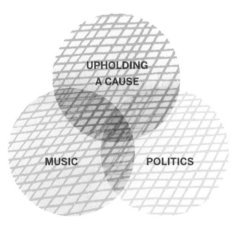

Jehmu Greene, **PRESIDENT OF ROCK THE VOTE**

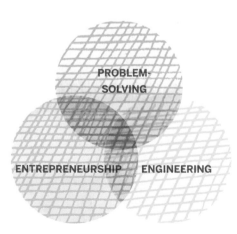

David Provost, **BUILDS SUBTERRANEAN FACILITIES FOR WINEMAKERS**

And keep in mind, like any good DJ, you won't play the same track forever. If you get tired of the song you're playing, swap a record out. Reflect, reassess, and, through trial and error, create a new mix that sounds right.

Consider Kary Mullis,* who loves chemistry. His road wasn't a single-point destination. It changed as his road took him in slightly different directions, from Berkeley to Kansas City, where he worked in pediatric cardiology, then back to San Francisco, where he began studying DNA. In the early 1990s, Kary's work with DNA replication led to a Nobel Prize. But even that is not a capstone on Kary's path.

"There are a few moments in your life—like say when you're called up on stage to get your Nobel Prize—that you say 'I think I did right,'" jokes Kary. "But then you say, 'Well, now what am I gonna do?' You have to have a little bit of confidence that the right thing will come along, and that you will see it when it does."

And that's the genius of living a life guided by your interests. One, those "right things" will occur more frequently, and two, you will be more attuned to noticing them when they do arrive. When you're off the Assembly Line and not consumed by the Noise, you can see your choices more clearly and balance the risks on their own terms. Since winning the Nobel Prize, Kary confides, "I've really changed my profession into something totally different. . . . My particular approach to life has been: I'm not anything. I'm me. I'm the sum total of all the things that I'm interested in, and I'm interested in a lot."

* **www.roadtripnation.com/leader/kary-mullis**

/ / / Roadmap / / /

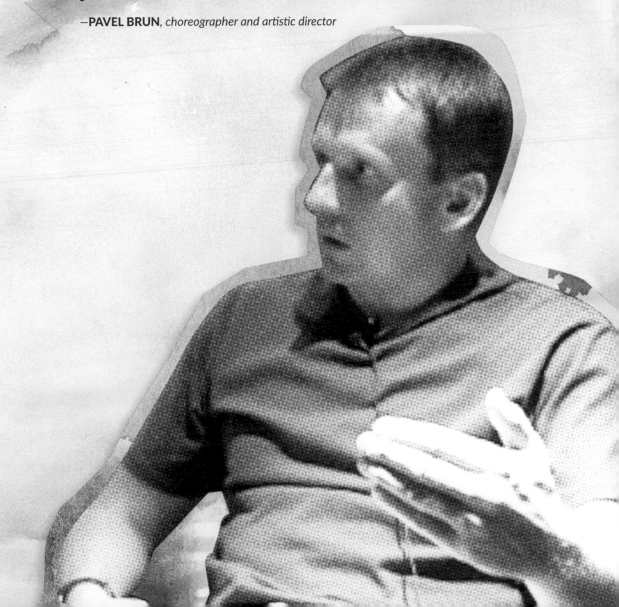

"Everything is the fusion. As long as you acknowledge existence of the fusion and as long as you are driven to find your own fusion, your own alchemy of elements, you'll be fine."

—**PAVEL BRUN**, *choreographer and artistic director*

EMBRACE THE MASHUP

When you're continually exploring your own interests, it's easier to find ways to remain engaged in your work. "You are talking to a forty-six-year-old person who is still thinking about what he wants to be when he grows up," says Pavel Brun,* the choreographer and artistic director who has choreographed shows for the Moscow Circus and spent nine years helping define the look and feel of Cirque du Soleil's influential stage shows.

Pavel takes the idea of the mashup to the extreme, continually willing to find new ways to manifest his interests. Schooling, external pressures, and influences were all secondary to Pavel's desire to explore new aspects of his love for live performance. That's how a self-described hippie living in the Soviet Union choreographing avant-garde theater pieces could end up, in the early 2000s, in Las Vegas, running a stage show for the mainstream grande dame of pop, Celine Dion. We call it two turntables and a microphone; Pavel calls it "the fusion," mixing different elements of your identity to create opportunity and experience.

We don't have to be as extreme as Pavel to make this strategy work. Let's say your Foundation is helping people, and your Core Interests are technology and medicine. Will your mix take you to hosting a radio show on scientific phenomena like Karl Kruszelnicki? Will you work to eradicate worldwide health epidemics like Google.org's Larry Brilliant? Maybe you'll implement and manage information software for a business to ensure the best return on cost and productivity, like Lillie Ng,* an IT architect for IBM. You could even be on the front line of medical breakthroughs, developing tools like the first print-to-speech reading machine for the blind, as inventor Ray Kurzweil did. All of these jobs

 * www.roadtripnation.com/leader/pavel-brun

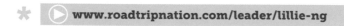 * www.roadtripnation.com/leader/lillie-ng

service the Foundation of helping people and two Core Interests (technology and medicine). Through action you get to know which is right for you. And if one isn't right, you simply swap out the record and mix again.

No matter how cynical you may be about all this, we really, truly are not just feeding you career guidance jargon. We have genuine proof that this strategy works.

One of the great aspects of amassing the proof is that in addition to reading about it here, you can go to our website, **www.roadtripnation.com/roadmap**, punch in your own Core Interests and Foundation, and discover Leaders who've crafted meaningful lives from the same set as yours. Swap out one Core Interest for another and watch how the song changes. Each time you make a change to a Core Interest or Foundation, you're looking at a different way to approach your life. Which combination sounds right to you?

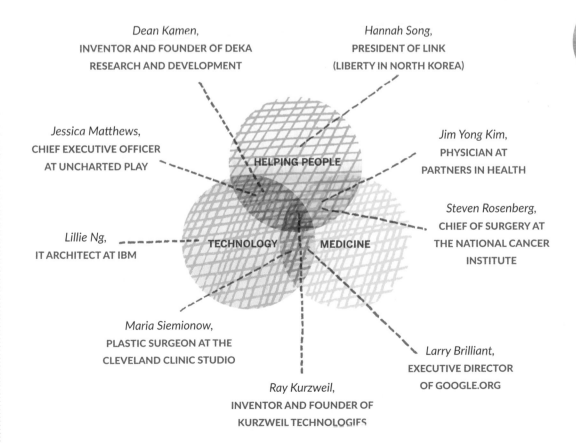

Dean Kamen,
INVENTOR AND FOUNDER OF DEKA
RESEARCH AND DEVELOPMENT

Hannah Song,
PRESIDENT OF LINK
(LIBERTY IN NORTH KOREA)

Jessica Matthews,
CHIEF EXECUTIVE OFFICER
AT UNCHARTED PLAY

Jim Yong Kim,
PHYSICIAN AT
PARTNERS IN HEALTH

HELPING PEOPLE

Steven Rosenberg,
CHIEF OF SURGERY AT
THE NATIONAL CANCER
INSTITUTE

Lillie Ng,
IT ARCHITECT AT IBM

TECHNOLOGY   MEDICINE

Maria Siemionow,
PLASTIC SURGEON AT THE
CLEVELAND CLINIC STUDIO

Ray Kurzweil,
INVENTOR AND FOUNDER OF
KURZWEIL TECHNOLOGIES

Larry Brilliant,
EXECUTIVE DIRECTOR
OF GOOGLE.ORG

What would some ideal-for-you mashups look like?

Take all the ideas you've had about your own road while reading this book and boil them down into a Foundation and two Core Interests. Revisit the Foundations on page 132 and the Core Interests on pages 122 to 123 and choose the ones that get you most excited. You don't have to commit to any one direction now; the goal is to identify all the combinations that you find compelling.

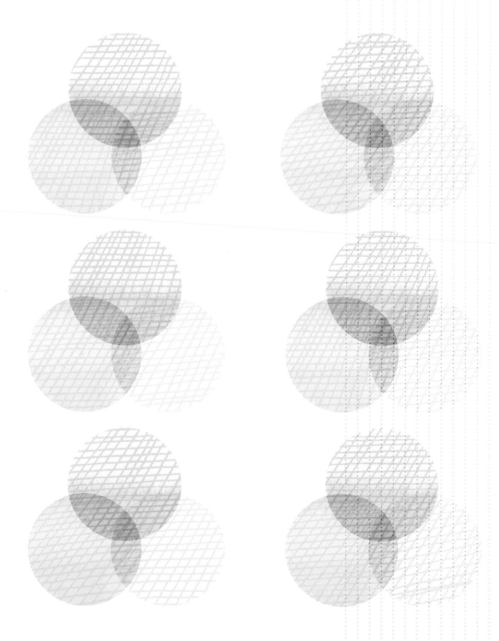

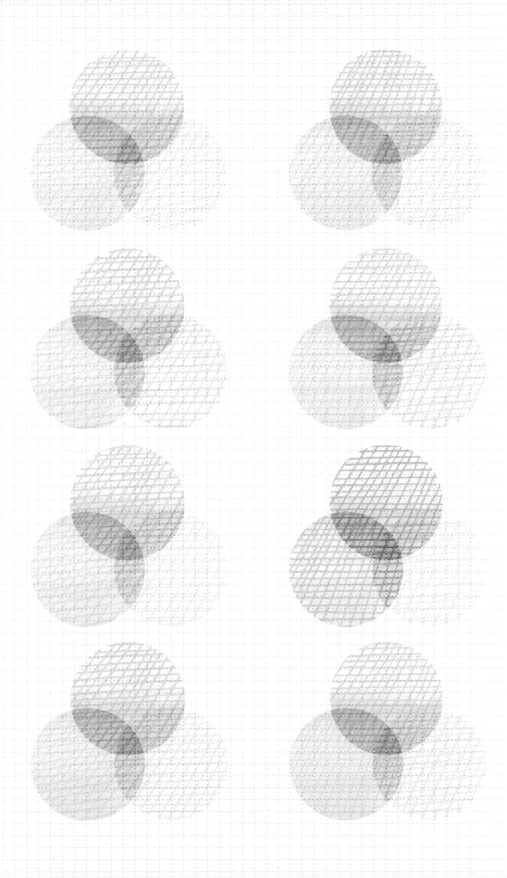

CHAPTER 11

YOU MIGHT NOT BE CRAZY, BUT MAYBE YOU SHOULD BE

The summer that Roadtripper Brooklyn Smith joined us on the Green RV started as one of exasperation for her. "I'm not sure how people do anything other than be a lawyer or a banker, which is what my parents sent me to college to be," she said.

Her parents had given her a pretty standard blueprint: "Just do something conventional. Make money. That's all you really need." The options she'd seen growing up in her Ohio hometown hadn't inspired her either. All she knew was she didn't want to follow the Assembly Line, but everything else just seemed . . . unknowable or unrealistic.

She hit the road with us with an eye on a goal: find those truly inspiring role models her life so far had sheltered her from. Were they out there? Were they successful? Were they happy? That summer Brooklyn did indeed find them, all over the country. People like the owners of a studio that crafts bikes from bamboo, the inventors of a soccer ball that generates electricity when it's kicked, the creators of a mobile film school, robotics engineers, civil rights lawyers, sculptors, brewers, kung-fu masters, and monks.

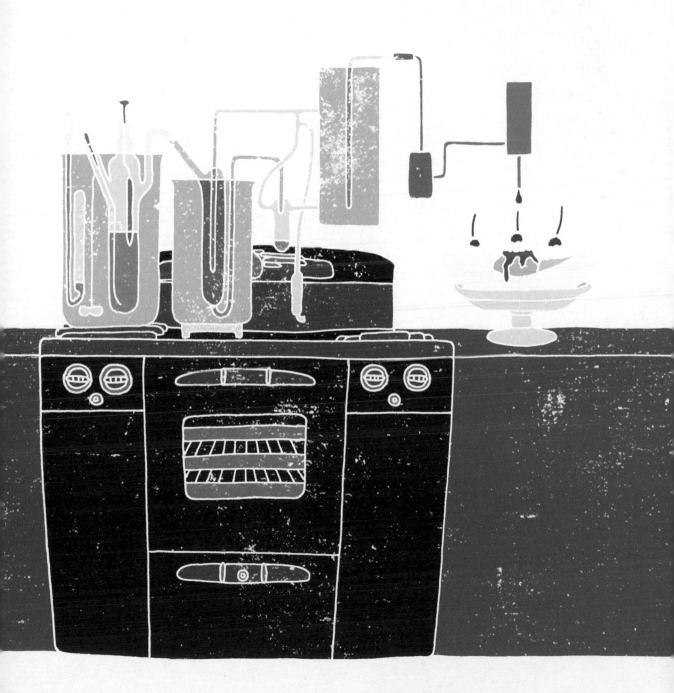

Brooklyn was astounded. "You're the people that I've been told don't exist!"

Those people, each of whom had a Worklife that was unheard-of or seemingly unrealistic, were thriving. Brooklyn's world had opened up.

EMBRACE PLAUSIBILITY

When we aspire to live a life fueled by our interests, the first hurdle we face is the basic notion of accepting its plausibility. Embracing the fact that our vision is possible can be enormously difficult in the face of everyday pressures and expectations, to say nothing of our own hampered worldviews. We are the sum of our experiences, and if our experiences haven't presented us with alternative paths, we'll tend to believe in only the path we can see. This is true no matter who you are. If your worldview never included the idea of becoming a lawyer or an engineer or street artist or an organic coffee roaster, those are going to seem like crazy options.

Think about blinders on a horse, like the cab horse teams in New York's Central Park. The blinders keep them on the straight-and-narrow path, ferrying gawking tourists from one corner of the park to the next, but they also act as insulation. If you take the blinders off the horse, the influx of stimuli could frighten and confuse the horse. So many choices! So many different directions to canter off to: the entirety of Manhattan, and the bridges and all that leads beyond them. That's what can happen to us when we take our own blinders off. At first it can feel overwhelming and intimidating.

Thanks to the myopic view we develop from the Assembly Line, we resist the very real possibility of doing things differently.

If, however, you can learn to question your own ideas about risk and safety, you can start to see what's Noise and what really is within your grasp. Entrepreneur Zach Kaplan was masterful at this perspective-altering approach when we met with him. Zach is the founder of Inventables, an online hardware store that enables industrial designers and other small-time garage entrepreneurs to order small quantities of materials and products—like 3-D printer supplies, suction-cup tape, and blank circuit boards—that typically are available only in bulk to large corporations. Zach started his business after seeing that the needs of individual designers and innovators weren't being met by the conventional infrastructure.

When we mentioned that starting a business seems inherently risky, Zach shot back, "Why is that risky?" Why, he questioned, would it be any more secure to work for an established company? What parameters had we developed that made us think in such a way? "If you think about it," Zach told us, "it's actually safer to start a business than to work at a big company, because in a small business, if you started it, you control the decision making. But if you work at a big company, you could do a great job and they could lay off twenty thousand people. You did a great job, but they laid you off because you were part of this department. So I'm not sure that it's necessarily less risky."

Zach's point isn't really as much about the judgment call of small business versus big business as it is about challenging perceived notions. His story shows us there are always multiple avenues to success.

Believing in the idea of multiple possibilities within our own lives is very difficult. We look at the rent due in a week, the endless bills, the plans for an upcoming vacation, the burgeoning family, or whatever the realities of our situation, and we balk. Combining our Foundation and our Core Interests into a dream job in Gumdrop Land might sound great, but it's all too easy to return to the notion that it's too crazy, too risky, too much of a pipe dream.

We're here to remind you it's not a pipe dream.

Be crazy.

Because it's not as crazy as you think.

THE BALLAD OF THE TURTLE WALKER

We often host events at schools, and one of our staple activities when we present to students involves getting them to think more broadly about where their futures might take them. We start by asking them to think of their dream jobs. We get back some sincere answers, and some joke answers from the meatballs in the back. Little do they know, the jokesters are actually playing right into our hands.

Once, we heard **"I wanna be a turtle walker!"** followed by an eruption of laughter from the group.

One of us replied, "What do you mean by turtle walker?" while another one of us hopped online, searching "turtle walker."

"You know, I want to be someone who takes people's turtles on walks, and makes sure they're getting enough exercise and stuff," the funny guy answered.

"Come on up here."

He came to the mic, loving the attention. He didn't love it so much when we handed him a phone with the number for a turtle rehabilitation center we'd looked up and implored him to call and ask about turtle exercise.

He turned beet red, but was good enough to play along, like the ham he was, and have an informative conversation about the ins and outs of turtle rehab with a real-life turtle walker at the Hidden Harbor Marine Environmental Project in Florida.

We've conducted this "You make up a job, we'll find you a phone number" exercise over and over again. It's a tried-and-true experiment that never fails to yield interesting and legitimate occupations.

IF YOU CAN DREAM IT UP, SOMEBODY IS PROBABLY GETTING A PAYCHECK FOR IT.

Here's a fun way to embrace what's possible. Take a look at the words below.
Circle three or four that grab your attention. The less related they are, the better.
Next, jump online and type the combination you chose into your search engine.

Teacher   Healing

Clock   Design   Vitamin B

Kite

Farm

Cat   Juice

Carving

Hamburger

Medicine   Los Angeles

Tractor

Fresco   Tax Return

Tour   Chocolate

Serving   Candles   Tokyo

Rope   Textile

Historian   Fashion   Wood

Bicycle

Canvas   Driving   Hotel

Free-Range

The goal is to find jobs, businesses, or professionals that include a mashup of
the words you circled. You might find an interesting article, a volunteer opportunity, a business you never expected to see, or someone you can approach
as a mentor. Maybe you'll find someone in a role that combines these words,
or maybe you'll even find your niche. The results should surprise you—they
definitely surprised us.

What interesting people, places, or things did you find by searching your word combination?

DISCOVERIES AND REFLECTIONS

The point, of course, isn't that you should take a Mad Libs approach to finding a livelihood. But what you might think is a ridiculous option is very likely work that puts food on somebody's table. In the face of the utterly bizarre and unexpected, how "crazy," really, are your own dreams?

Skeptical friends and family, for example, besieged Peter Lynn* when he decided to devote his engineering skills to making kites. On the surface, kite making can seem trifling, but it's based on real skills and real-world demand for entertainment, beauty, surprise, and play—all of which people will pay for. Now the owner of a beloved worldwide kite brand based in New Zealand, and one of the premier creators and suppliers of innovative designs for kites and kiteboards, Peter's success is a perfect example of how crazy becomes feasible when we follow our interests.

  www.roadtripnation.com/leader/peter-lynn

"You can make a living and still follow your hobbies, even if you do the smallest thing. If you don't do anything else, and you just concentrate on it, and you do it forever, there will be a place in the world for it. It doesn't matter how small a thing it is. The world is big enough for these small niches to be a life."

—**PETER LYNN**, *kite maker, engineer, and inventor*

There's nothing wrong with following a traditional path, but you'll find deeper satisfaction when you tweak the expected to support your unique self. Take Elise Benstein.* She's a scientist. You can't get more traditional than that, but Elise took her science background and became a real-life Willy Wonka, veering from the norm by working for the candy manufacturer Jelly Belly to create new flavors. "I'm at the forefront of developing new candy products and . . . I never thought I would be doing that." Elise combined her love of science and food and is now being paid to create such wacky confections as the vomit-flavored jelly beans in the company's Harry Potter Bertie Bott's Every Flavour Beans. Elise advised us to be open to capturing those opportunities when they present themselves and embracing new concepts.

Here are a few more custom-tailored livelihoods we've come across:

CORPORATE MANAGEMENT + HEAVY METAL = *Terry Stewart,*
CEO OF THE ROCK AND ROLL HALL OF FAME AND MUSEUM

PRIMATES + GERIATRICS = *Raven Jackson,*
RESIDENT VETERINARIAN AT CHIMP HAVEN, *a retirement community for chimpanzees*

FOOD + POLITICS = *Andy Shallal,*
OWNER OF BUSBOYS AND POETS, *a restaurant, bookstore, and community gathering place that encourages diversity in the discussion of art, politics, and culture*

TATTOOING + TRAVEL = *Kitty Love,*
TRAVELING TATTOO ARTIST

  www.roadtripnation.com/leader/elise-benstein

As you look at your own life, don't limit yourself in imagining the ways that your interests can manifest. William Morris, a renowned glassblower and successful niche builder, challenged us with this hypothetical: "Would you rather have one year of utter vitality or ten years of just ho-hum mediocrity? You know, either choice is fine! But just be the choice that you make. Be it! Don't make the choice of vitality and live mediocrity." In other words, once you've realized you want to live true to your interests, don't hold back. Take a moment right now and look back at the combinations of Foundation and Core Interests you chose in the previous chapter. Did you really set yourself free to imagine? Did you cast your net wide enough to capture all the wild opportunities available to you, like Elise did, using a science degree to dream up zany candy flavors? For a moment, just let the external and internal naysayers fade away and ask yourself:

What's my vomit-flavored jelly bean?

THE INTERNAL GPS

By Willie Witte

THE WORD "LOST" WAS TAKING ON A NEW MEANING FOR ME. I FOUND MYSELF WAKING UP REGULARLY IN THE MIDDLE OF THE NIGHT, SQUINTING INTO THE DARKNESS, AND WONDERING, "WHERE AM I?" I WOULD SLOWLY REGAIN CONSCIOUSNESS, THE DIMLY LIT WALLS COMING INTO FOCUS AND RESTORING A VAGUE SENSE OF FAMILIARITY. I WAS, OF COURSE, IN MY TEMPORARY HOME ON WHEELS, A BIG GREEN RV.

ONE MORNING, NOT LONG AFTER I'D FINALLY SETTLED BACK INTO SLEEP, MY CELL PHONE ALARM STARTED TO BUZZ, WAKING ME FOR ANOTHER LEG OF OUR JOURNEY. I FISHED THROUGH THE COUCH CUSHIONS TO FIND MY PHONE AND GLANCED AT THE DATE ON ITS SCREEN: JULY 21. WE'D BEEN OUT ON THE ROAD TWENTY-EIGHT DAYS.

HOW PEOPLE SURVIVED BEFORE GPS IS BEYOND ME. BY THIS STAGE OF OUR TRIP I'D REACHED A SPECIAL LEVEL OF DISORIENTA-TION, A KIND OF LAND-BORNE JET LAG I'D DEVELOPED BY HAVING TO

Willie Witte's business card reads "Professional Roadtripper." Seriously, it does. With more than 50,000 miles clocked in Roadtrip Nation's Green RV, he has now set foot in 49 of the 50 United States (someday he'll make it to North Dakota!). More important, as a cameraman for the Roadtrip Nation television series he has been behind the lens for nearly 200 interviews with inspiring people from all walks of life. When Willie was on the Roadtrip he describes here, he had recently left his small hometown of Sandpoint, Idaho, and was filming a team of Roadtrippers from the similarly small town of Stevensville, Montana. Five years later, Willie still regards this experience as one of the most impactful in his life.

NAVIGATE THE STREETS OF A NEW LOCATION EVERY TWO OR THREE DAYS. THE MAMMOTH CAVE IN KENTUCKY. IT HAD BEEN KNOXVILLE BEFORE THAT, AND BEFORE THAT ATLANTA, NEW ORLEANS, AUSTIN, SANTA FE, ROSWELL, SEDONA, AND LOS ANGELES. ON JULY 21 IT WAS CLEVELAND, AND WE WERE, ONCE AGAIN, LOST.

"OH, WAIT," I STUTTERED FROM THE PASSENGER SEAT, "THIS THING IS TELLING US WE'RE GOING THE WRONG WAY. HOLD ON." IT'S NO SURPRISE WE WERE OFF TRACK, CONSIDERING MOST OF US IN THE RV HAD NEVER BEEN EAST OF THE MISSISSIPPI BEFORE. I WATCHED AS THE GPS RECALIBRATED.

"YEAH, UM . . . SORRY, WE NEED TO TURN AROUND."

MY FATIGUE, HOWEVER, WENT DEEPER THAN THE GRIND OF THE ROAD. AFTER WEEKS ON THE ROAD, THE MENTAL BURNOUT FACTOR IS REAL, BUT THERE WAS A SIDE TO IT THAT WAS THE BEST KIND OF EXHAUSTION POSSIBLE. IT GREW FROM THE SATURATION OF STORIES AND WISDOM WE'D BEEN SOAKING UP AT EACH STOP. LIKE EVERYONE ELSE ON THE TRIP, I'D GROWN UP IN MY OWN BUBBLE THAT WAS SLOWLY STARTING TO BURST. RAISED IN A RURAL COUNTRY TOWN, MY ROADMAP HAD BEEN CLEARLY DEFINED BY THE NOISE, BOLDLY MARKED WITH PLENTY OF "DO NOT CROSS" LINES THAT TOLD ME WHERE I DIDN'T BELONG, WHAT I WAS NOT CAPABLE OF, AND WHAT I SHOULD BE AFRAID OF TRYING. MY OWN FEVERED MIND HAD DRAWN A FEW OF THOSE LINES ITSELF.

BUT OUT HERE ON THE ROAD, ABSORBING STORY AFTER STORY, THOSE LINES WERE STARTING TO DIMINISH. THE BIG QUESTION EMERGING NOW WAS: WITHOUT ALL THESE BORDERS, HOW AM I SUPPOSED TO KNOW WHERE TO GO NEXT?

THE MAN WE WERE EN ROUTE TO MEET THIS OVERCAST CLEVELAND MORNING PROMISED TO BE A WELCOME ADDITION TO THIS CHOIR OF NEW VOICES IN MY HEAD. UP TO THIS POINT, OUR ONLY KNOWLEDGE OF HIM CAME FROM A MAGAZINE ARTICLE ABOUT THE MOST INTERESTING PEOPLE IN CLEVELAND. THE SHORT BIO WENT LIKE THIS: VAN TAYLOR MONROE IS A CUSTOM SHOE ARTIST. HE HANDPAINTS TENNIS SHOES. FOR MONEY. HIS CLIENTS INCLUDE WILL.I.AM, T.I., AND P. DIDDY. ONE OF HIS WORKS, A PAIR OF NIKE AIR FORCE 1S FEATURING AN ICONIC

IMAGE OF BARACK OBAMA, WILL BE ON DISPLAY AT THE SMITHSONIAN NATIONAL MUSEUM OF AFRICAN-AMERICAN HISTORY AND CULTURE IN WASHINGTON, DC. WHERE DID THIS GUY COME FROM? HOW EXACTLY DOES ONE CREATE A SUSTAINABLE LIFE IN THE TENNIS SHOE-PAINTING BUSINESS?

VAN WAS WAITING FOR US IN THE COURTYARD OF THE TOWER CITY CENTER, A MALL IN DOWNTOWN CLEVELAND. HE HANDED ME A PAIR OF AIR JORDANS WITH AN IMMACULATE RENDERING OF LEBRON JAMES ON THEM. MY FIRST REACTION WAS THAT I COULDN'T BELIEVE THE SHOES WERE HAND-PAINTED, AND AFTER VAN ASSURED ME THEY WERE, MY SECOND REACTION WAS TO SET THEM DOWN FOR FEAR OF SMUDGING HIS MASTERPIECES.

"I WAS BORN AN ARTIST," HE TOLD US. BUT WHEN COLLEGE CAME AROUND, VAN PURSUED A BUSINESS DEGREE INSTEAD, LANDING HIM, POST COLLEGE, AS AN UPWARDLY MOBILE ACCOUNT EXEC FOR A LOGISTICS FIRM IN CINCINNATI.

"MY PASSION WASN'T THERE, BUT THAT WAS WHERE THE MONEY WAS AT," VAN SAID. "AND I'M THINKING THIS IS HOW I'LL PAY THE BILLS AND HAVE A FAMILY. I'M JUST GOING TO PAINT ON THE SIDE." IT WAS, UP TO THIS POINT, A FAMILIAR STORY. THAT BALANCE BETWEEN OUR AUTHENTIC INTERESTS AND A NEED TO PAY THE BILLS IS A CONSTANT STRUGGLE—AND WE ALL KNOW THAT SOCIETY TAKES THE "EITHER/OR" APPROACH, USUALLY FAVORING THE OR SIDE. AT THE FIRM, VAN COULDN'T FOCUS. HE COULDN'T EVEN PICK UP THE PHONE TO FOLLOW

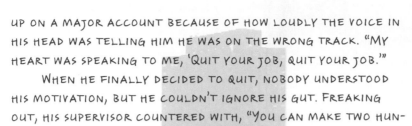

UP ON A MAJOR ACCOUNT BECAUSE OF HOW LOUDLY THE VOICE IN HIS HEAD WAS TELLING HIM HE WAS ON THE WRONG TRACK. "MY HEART WAS SPEAKING TO ME, 'QUIT YOUR JOB, QUIT YOUR JOB.'"

WHEN HE FINALLY DECIDED TO QUIT, NOBODY UNDERSTOOD HIS MOTIVATION, BUT HE COULDN'T IGNORE HIS GUT. FREAKING OUT, HIS SUPERVISOR COUNTERED WITH, "YOU CAN MAKE TWO HUN-DRED THOUSAND DOLLARS A YEAR HERE, AND YOU ARE GOING TO QUIT TO BECOME AN ARTIST?" BUT THAT'S WHAT VAN DID. I FELT A CHILL RUN DOWN MY ARMS. I REMEMBER LOOKING ACROSS THE TABLE AND THINKING, IS THIS GUY FOR REAL? $200K IS NO JOKE! I ASKED MYSELF THE DIFFICULT QUESTION: COULD I LEAVE THAT KIND OF MONEY ON THE TABLE AND JUMP WITHOUT A SAFETY NET? MY ANSWER (NO WAY) GAVE ME A NEW LEVEL OF RESPECT FOR THE CONVICTIONS OF THE ARTIST SITTING IN FRONT OF ME.

"BUT I NEVER THOUGHT IT WOULD GET AS BAD AS IT GOT," VAN CONTINUED. HE WAS PAINTING CANVAS, PAINTING ANYTHING HE COULD, BUT WAS UNABLE TO MAKE A VIABLE LIVING. THINGS WERE LOOKING GRIM, BUT WITH YOUNGER SIBLINGS AND LITTLE COUSINS LOOKING UP TO HIM, HE DECIDED NOT TO LET ANYONE KNOW WHAT HE WAS FACING.

"IDEAS ARE LIKE BABIES," HE TOLD US, "THEY NEED TIME TO DEVELOP IN SECRET, IN THE WOMB, BEFORE THEY CAN SURVIVE OUT IN THE WORLD." I CONSIDERED THE LIST OF "IDEA BABIES" I WAS HARBORING IN MY OWN MIND.

"January comes around, and I got an eviction notice on my door," said Van. But Van wasn't ready to throw in the towel. Again, he thought of the example he needed to set for his family. "If I was homeless for a while, I was gonna get back on my feet, and I was gonna make this a success story." This was 2008, a tough year for anyone to find work, let alone an artist. It helped that Barack Obama's voice and encouraging message were infiltrating psyches. One night, Van woke from a dream with a rush of inspiration, and decided to paint the president-to-be a pair of Nikes he had lying around. He took a picture and posted it online, saying he didn't think much of it.

The shoe went viral. First it sprawled across the blogosphere, and then appeared on the news networks.

Smiling at the irony, Van told us of the rush of recognition the shoe brought. "I was in the Wall Street Journal. The Wall Street Journal! With a painted tennis shoe!" I imagined the faces of Van's former coworkers at the logistics firm, opening their journals at their cubicles, seeing Van and his shoe. Triumph!

From there, Van's name gained notice and the celebrities began wearing his shoes to high-profile events. Even President Obama owns two pairs of Van's custom shoes. Van had, indeed, made it a success story. But how? What did it take? Before the rappers and basketball players were blowing up his phone, before the media and the museums were tracking him down, when he was quitting his steady job and, later, preparing to be evicted, how did he know this would happen? How did he know it would work out?

Van explained, "Your heart is like a GPS system. A GPS system in your car will tell you where to go, but it won't turn your car for you. You're going somewhere you don't know, looking around saying, 'Alright! I hope this knows what it's talking about!'" Now he was speaking my language. I must have been nodding my head like an idiot because all I could

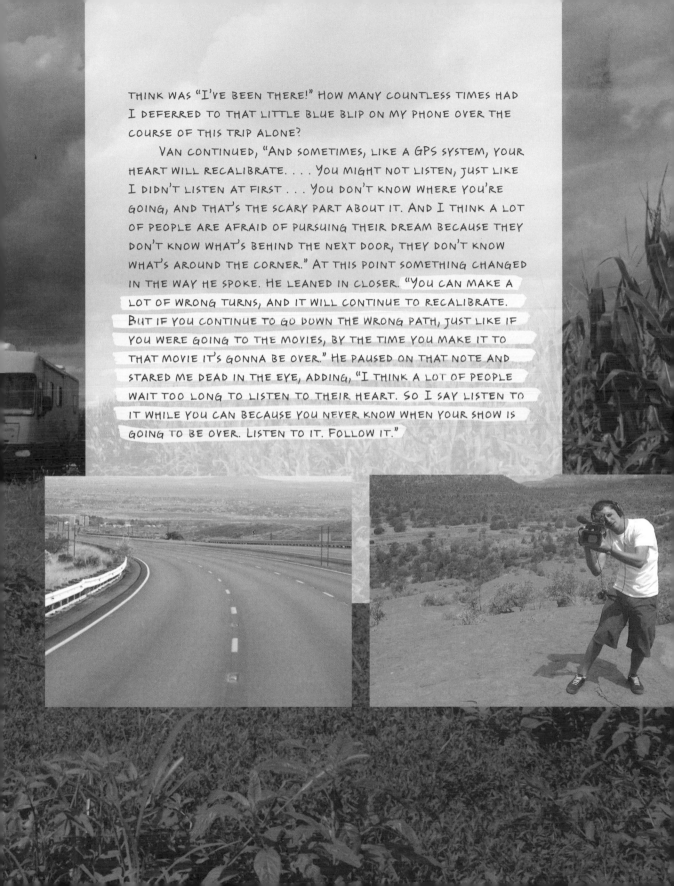

THINK WAS "I'VE BEEN THERE!" HOW MANY COUNTLESS TIMES HAD
I DEFERRED TO THAT LITTLE BLUE BLIP ON MY PHONE OVER THE
COURSE OF THIS TRIP ALONE?

VAN CONTINUED, "AND SOMETIMES, LIKE A GPS SYSTEM, YOUR
HEART WILL RECALIBRATE. . . . YOU MIGHT NOT LISTEN, JUST LIKE
I DIDN'T LISTEN AT FIRST . . . YOU DON'T KNOW WHERE YOU'RE
GOING, AND THAT'S THE SCARY PART ABOUT IT. AND I THINK A LOT
OF PEOPLE ARE AFRAID OF PURSUING THEIR DREAM BECAUSE THEY
DON'T KNOW WHAT'S BEHIND THE NEXT DOOR, THEY DON'T KNOW
WHAT'S AROUND THE CORNER." AT THIS POINT SOMETHING CHANGED
IN THE WAY HE SPOKE. HE LEANED IN CLOSER. "YOU CAN MAKE A
LOT OF WRONG TURNS, AND IT WILL CONTINUE TO RECALIBRATE.
BUT IF YOU CONTINUE TO GO DOWN THE WRONG PATH, JUST LIKE IF
YOU WERE GOING TO THE MOVIES, BY THE TIME YOU MAKE IT TO
THAT MOVIE IT'S GONNA BE OVER." HE PAUSED ON THAT NOTE AND
STARED ME DEAD IN THE EYE, ADDING, "I THINK A LOT OF PEOPLE
WAIT TOO LONG TO LISTEN TO THEIR HEART. SO I SAY LISTEN TO
IT WHILE YOU CAN BECAUSE YOU NEVER KNOW WHEN YOUR SHOW IS
GOING TO BE OVER. LISTEN TO IT. FOLLOW IT."

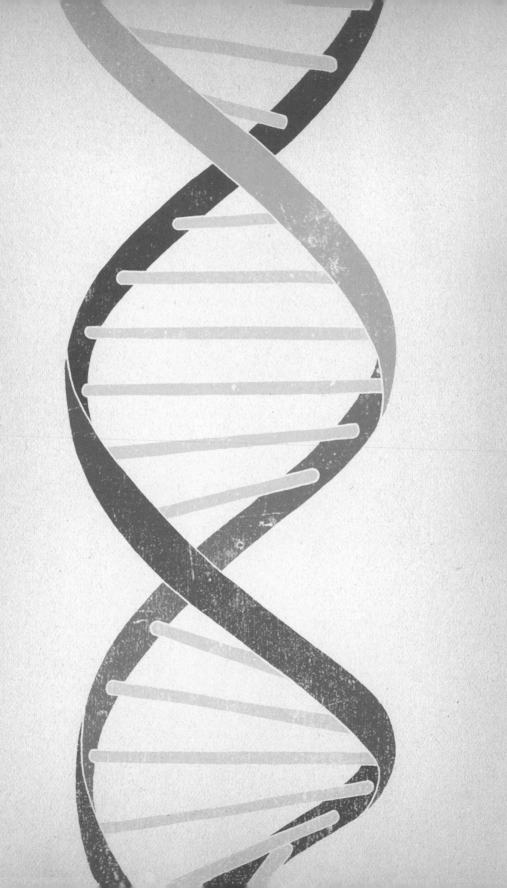

CHAPTER 12

WHAT ARE YOUR SUBJECTIVE TRUTHS?

Most of us agree on the big truths in life: murder is wrong, you shouldn't steal, it's good to help old ladies cross the street, you should never order fish on an airplane. Those are easy, but what about the things that are true to us and us only? We each have a set of defining parameters that speak to the core of who we are—these are our Subjective Truths. And the ways they interact with our Foundation and our Core Interests is important.

TRUTHS	SUBJECTIVE TRUTHS
- Without water, we will die.	- I want to make a lot of money.
- Camels have three eyelids.	- Starting a family and spending time with them is of paramount importance.
- Economic bubbles will burst; job markets are cyclical.	- I thrive best in the structure and security of the business world.
- Karaoke means "empty orchestra" in Japanese.	- I work best when I'm my own boss.
- The Ms in M&Ms stand for "Mars and Murrie," the last names of the company's founders.	- I hate big cities.
- There are multiple ways to build a life around your interests.	- I need to live in a city.
- The term "jorts" is a portmanteau of the words "jeans" and "shorts."	- Jorts are both a gift and a plague to the human race.

Subjective Truths are like the sieve in a gold-mining pan. As you shake the possibilities around, your Subjective Truths will let the ideas you can't roll with fall through, leaving you with the gold—the possibilities that feel right because they agree with who you are.

Some of your Subjective Truths will be evident immediately, but others may not be revealed until you're staring them in the face. Such was the case for Nathan, one of the original Roadtrippers and a cofounder of Roadtrip Nation. "My freak-out," Nathan remembers, "began at a career fair at college." After listening to the Noise and shelving an early dream of being an artist, Nathan had done a stint at a local junior college, taken some business courses, and transferred over to a four-year university to earn his degree as a business major. "I was too passive, not asking myself the important questions. I just accepted that business students become business consultants. That was the path." And Nathan was on it.

At the job fair, Nathan met the people who were at the other end of his Assembly Line. "It was all these super well-dressed career people representing the top-tier consulting companies. I passed around my résumé, even though I really had no clue what this job was I was applying for. So I asked one of the consultants if I could take him out to lunch and learn a little about what he did."

While they ate and talked, Nathan asked a question: "So, do you have to wear a suit every day?"

"Well, yeah," the consultant responded. "But I love wearing suits—wearing nice clothes. We even get a clothing budget, so it's pretty great."

"My response," recalls Nathan, "and I don't even know if I could call it a response as much as a gut reaction, was, 'This is not me. I am not a suit-and-tie guy. Weddings and funerals. That's where I draw the line.'"

Once he had claimed that Subjective Truth as his own, Nathan's path instantly changed. A huge portion of the jobs that a business major would aspire to were immediately dropped from Nathan's range of possibilities. The sieve of the Subjective Truths had just washed away the ill-suited choices, leaving Nathan with opportunities more in tune with his values.

YOUR SUBJECTIVE TRUTHS ARE CALLING

The point isn't "suits bad, T-shirts good." It's that we each have to listen to our own Subjective Truths, because every Subjective Truth matters, and making choices against them will result in dissatisfaction and frustration down the line. It also gives us perspective on other people's choices and motivations: We all place things differently on the Subjective Truth spectrum. Understanding whether we're happiest working within a corporate structure or in a small business, or out tilling a field, are all components of living a life guided by our own truths.

"I went through hell trying to retain my own life," remembers the wonderfully nutty Barry Brickell,* a potter, author, artist, and (believe it or not) railway conductor, who operates a pottery studio and popular narrow-gauge railroad that winds through a gorgeous patch of land in the rural mountains of New Zealand. "I started making pottery at age fourteen, right through university. I was not a good academic, but I was told by my mother and father I had to get a degree from a university so that I could have a successful career. But I wanted to be a potter and make pots. My father was horrified and shocked and said, 'You'll never be able to bring up a family and have a nice wife and give me lots of grandchildren if you're going to be a potter.'"

  www.roadtripnation.com/leader/barry-brickell

With a tinge of mock rage Barry replied, "But I don't want a nice wife. I don't want to make lots of grandchildren for you. I want to make pots!" Barry, from his studio in the dense forests of New Zealand, laughs at the memory, but his story holds something special. Barry's Subjective Truths were clear, and although he did get his degree and tried his hand at a "normal" profession, he quickly gave it up. The standard model of an adult life, with a spouse and children and a picket-fenced yard, was out the window for Barry, for better or worse. He was, no other way to put it, a potter. Barry's Subjective Truths informed his vision and guided his interests. This led him down curious paths, including native forest restoration and, along with his pottery, founding the Driving Creek Railway—a personally operated railway that is part playground, part scenic tour, and part art installation. All of it is a lasting testament to his resolve to stay true to himself.

"I wasted as much money as I could, buying rails and timber and steel beams for bridges," he recalls of the enormous amount of work it took to create the railway that runs through the pristine mountainside forest and is now one of the most well-known tourist attractions in New Zealand. "I've got four drivers

now, and that means I can stay in my 'asylum,' my studio, and make pots, which is what I've always wanted to do. My father, if he could see this setup now, he would do a double take, wouldn't he?"

As we know, the Noise is pernicious. It sneaks in, and it has a way of implanting ideas in our brain that might actually conflict with our Subjective Truths. No matter how we were raised—rich, poor, religious, hippie-commune–style—we'll be exposed to values and ideas that, if we take the time to think about them, might not actually be ours. This can even happen later in life as well, in the culture of our jobs or schooling or family life. Differentiating between what's authentically your truth and what's societal Noise takes some digging, and some good old-fashioned resistance.

John Passacantando, the executive director of Greenpeace USA, deeply understands this. It began at an early age, when John's parents gave him a great gift by telling him, "We don't care what you do, just so long as you do your best at it." Simple words, but they hold a remarkable power.

"Try to drop the dogma that you get, even from your own peers," John urges. "That stuff is always somebody else's agenda, and it won't help you, and it will never speak to your heart. Whether something is good or bad to do should be based on how it feels to you and your own sense of ethics, not somebody else's rule book. If you feel passionately about doing conservative political work, you should do that. If you feel passionately about working for the companies that I think are pillaging the earth, you should do that, and you should do the best job you can for them. And you shouldn't let somebody else judge you, as you follow your own path; that dogma can get you off course, but your own heart will never set you astray."

Subjective Truths are just that: subjective. We can't judge them, or pretend to understand what they mean outside of our own experience, but if we respect our own truths, we end up moving in directions that will feel intrinsically satisfying. My Harrison, a section chief in the FBI, went from poverty to the halls of government by following her own need for stability, something her childhood lacked. "I grew up very poor in the housing projects in Tampa," My says. "I knew I wanted to get out of the projects. That was my ultimate goal. I knew that everything I did was for a purpose—a specific purpose. Growing up in the conditions I grew up in, you learn that drive. Nothing stands in your way."

YOUR SUBJECTIVE TRUTHS ARE YOUR VALUE SYSTEM

Respecting your Subjective Truths is about creating a life you want to live without compromising your values. Your Subjective Truths all add up to a unique value system that will inform your important decisions. For some of us, a strong sense of moral rectitude might bar us from working for a company whose practices we disagree with. Others might be completely content at that same company for the great pay, health insurance, and kick-ass company parties. Maybe the size of a company is most important to you, and you thrive most in a close-knit, family-style environment where everyone knows that you hate soy milk in your coffee. Or maybe you're just at your best when you're working from home, typing away in sweatpants. It might even be something visceral that turns you off a pathway, like hating the feeling of being in a hospital (Mike, original Roadtripper and cofounder of Roadtrip Nation, who was studying to be a doctor, luckily realized this before it was too late). Either way, it's up to us to determine what we value. There will always be someone out there who disagrees, but the point is: who cares? You're the one who has to live your life.

You'll find that some Subjective Truths outweigh the power of others. Knowing that spending extra time with your family is a louder Subjective Truth than the $10K more per year you'd earn at a more demanding job will help you say "Thanks, but no thanks," when the wrong offer pops up (and "Yes, please!" when the right one does). Your task is to listen to the value system that brings you satisfaction and weigh what works best for you. Money might be the most obvious factor in balancing your Subjective Truths. How much money do you need?

Consider our ragtag fleet of old RVs. Most TV production companies would trick theirs out with slick paint jobs and top-of-the-line built-in Jacuzzis. We chose to repurpose used RVs we found on Craigslist and paint them with on-sale house paint and hand rollers that cost less than a cup of coffee. Our priority of saving money here keeps more gas in our tanks and allows us to have more of the conversations and experiences that we value. "Experiences over paint jobs" is one of our Subjective Truths, and while it might not be right for MTV, it's right for us.

We all have those kinds of deep-seated truths—and they will be wildly different for all of us—but to make them useful they need to be examined and understood. Then, when it's time to pull out the old "for or against" ledger, you can make decisions about your path that will keep you in tune with your values.

If you think about it, every moment of your life is actually one of those "for or against" moments. Every day, we make decisions that are informed by our values; we just don't think about it that often. But the power in being able to say, definitively, "No, I don't want _____ in my life" or "Yes, I need to do _____ to be satisfied" is huge. It's what will lead you to your Open Road.

The struggle to understand and use our Subjective Truths is one that many of the Leaders have dealt with. Take a look at how the life paths of the following Leaders were guided by the values and vision derived from their Subjective Truths.

DEON CLARK
was a nuclear engineer

↓

Is it important that your work has a social impact?

YES   NO

↓

Founded a non-profit to help underserved youth.

VAN TAYLOR MONROE

was an account executive

Is it important to make a lot of money?

YES   NO

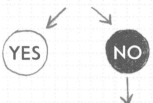

Quit his job to find a way to paint for a living.

CHRISTINA HEYNIGER

was a management consultant

Do you need to be in touch with nature?

YES   NO

Started her own adventure tourism consulting firm.

GRAEME RAE

was a professor of engineering

Would you prefer to wear a T-shirt all day?

YES   NO

Took his high-tech skills (and his T-shirts) to Surfline.

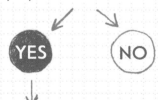
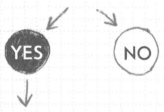

What are some of your Subjective Truths?

Do I want to work
independently?

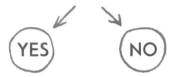

Do I need to be in touch
with nature?

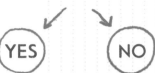

Do I need to make a lot
of money?

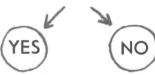

Does financial security drive
my decisions?

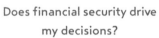

Is it important for my work to
have a social impact?

Would I give up security to take
a risk that *might* pan out?

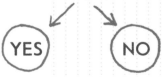

Would I rather dress casually
at work?

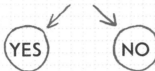

Do I need a lot of
structure?

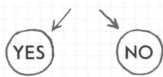

Does what I do in my career have
to match my personal beliefs?

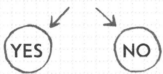

Do I want to stay near
my hometown?

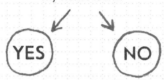

Do I care about having a
long commute?

Do I need to be physically
active in my job?

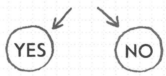

Do I want a job that allows me to
spend a lot of time with family?

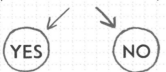

Would I rather live in
a city?

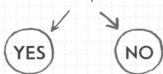

CHAPTER 13
SKILLS PAY BILLS

Let's not forget the nitty-gritty: Unless you're continually finding bags full of money on the street, you will need to get paid. It's easy for us to say "define your own road," and "do what you love," but we know you can't simply explore your interests and flit through life. You have to keep the lights on and pay off your credit cards. Life's necessities generally cost money, and there's no way around it. It's this cold, hard fact that keeps many of us on the Assembly Line.

And though paying the bills is both noble and right, there are sustainable ways to marry what we like to do with what we have to do and build a sustainable Worklife. If you think about it, your economic viability is like an engine in a car. But it's only the engine—not the *entire car*. The car won't go anywhere without an engine, of course, but an engine isn't going to hurtle forward on its own, either.

The best cars—those sleek automobiles we see hugging a winding mountain road in a car commercial—are not just about the engine. From the wheels and the suspension to the door handles, it is all these parts working in harmony that make the magic of the automobile. And the same is true about our lives. Making a ton of money with no meaning in the effort is like having a Lamborghini engine inside a Pinto with no working air-conditioning and windows that roll down only halfway. You can't revel in the ride, because the sum of the parts doesn't balance out. Conversely, "following your passion" with no way to feed yourself is akin to a car without an engine—broken down on the road to the

land of unicorns and rainbows. The trick to keeping the car rolling comfortably is finding a way to hitch an Economic Engine to what you love.

LOVE + MAKING MONEY = POSSIBLE

Mixing what you love with how you make money is a process that can seem daunting—and starting it *now* can seem frighteningly mistimed, especially when you have rent to pay. But the important thing to remember is, it can be done, and not just by the lucky few. From a pure "I don't want to move back in with my folks because they drive me freakin' crazy" perspective, the power of this book hinges on this chapter.

The gist of it is: You can build a career aligned with who you are as an individual, and you can make money doing it.

There are, however, a few hurdles on that path. The first is probably obvious: to get paid for something, it helps to be skilled at it.

When we talk about skills, we don't mean magical abilities. If your Foundation is your skeleton, and your Core Interests are the nervous system that sends the impulses that get you moving, your skills are the muscles, the heavy lifters that cause locomotion. And like real-life muscles, skills need to be exercised and developed. Your skills are built by activities and challenges that feed into your Foundation and Core Interests, but all of these things have to work together. You could be inherently skilled at logical, ordered thinking, but if you have zero interest in JavaScript or spending hours plotting out code, your skills would be wasted as a web developer.

So, back to the first hurdle. How do you get "good" at something? How do you develop skills in line with your Core Interests? You begin with what you love. Or what you like, if you have yet to figure out what you *love*. You just need to be engaged by something that interests you enough to put in the initial work. Your natural inclinations will guide you over the first hurdles. This isn't the end by any means, but it's the start. Before you know whether you're (potentially) good at something, you have to try it.

Gary Rydstrom, a seven-time Oscar-winning sound designer at Skywalker Sound, didn't really know he had a talent for sound design until he tried it: "You don't know how good you are at things until you try them, which is why you have to be led by your passion—if you're intrigued by something, it means you'll put the energy into being good at it. But to be naturally good at things now is impossible."

EXPERIENCE PERPETUAL MOTION

We might know what we're good at, but to Gary's point, it's more likely that we develop what we're good at as we genuinely explore what we're interested in. It's a perpetual-motion situation—your interest in something drives you to develop your skills in it, not the other way around. It's important to start with what you're interested in so that as you layer on your skills the two will come together in the right way. Just because you're skilled in math doesn't mean you need to learn to love crunching numbers at an accounting firm. Better to start with your interest in sports and then layer on your skill in math to end up running the stats for the Lakers. You start with your interests, develop skills, and then see what happens. Rinse and repeat. Rinse and repeat. Beta. Beta. Beta.

It's all about self-driven growth. "Even the stuff you're really good at, you're not necessarily really good at right away," says Ira Glass,* the host of *This American Life*. Ira is one of the main voices of public radio these days. His program, syndicated to more than five hundred radio stations, with millions more listeners online, ushered in a new wave of journalistic storytelling. Ira himself is,

✳   www.roadtripnation.com/leader/ira-glass

/// Skills Pay Bills ///

of course, a master storyteller and—as befitting a good interviewer—a great listener. But was he always? Is that how he began? Where did he get the chops? When we asked this, he paused for a moment, looking around in his recording booth, and said, "The key thing, I think, is to just force yourself through the work, to put yourself in the position where you have to turn out product. That's what will force the skills to come."

The revolving dance between skills and interests is, as Ira says, the hardest part of the process. Your confidence will be shaken, you will fail, you will question your desire to do the work and doubt your abilities. When one of his fellow producers from *This American Life* listened to material from Ira's early days, she jabbed, "Wow. There was no sign you had any talent at all. There wasn't even a hint you'd be any good." Ira takes comfort in the fact that "fortunately, things happen in stages. I was a terrible reporter, but I was still perfectly good at certain parts of working on the radio. I was an especially good editor, and in a way, that's the best part of my job now." Ira's skill as an editor intersected with his desire to explore radio storytelling, and of course, the more he did it, the better he became as both an editor and an on-air personality.

Is there a flip side to this? What if it just seems like you can't cut it, no matter how much work you put in? Even Ira admits that there are times where you just have to cut your losses and get out. If the skills you have or the skills you are trying to develop simply cannot align with your interests (or pay enough) no matter how hard you try, it may be time to change.

But this doesn't mean abandoning your interests entirely; it just means changing your perspective. Just because you're ill-suited to one pathway within your interests doesn't mean that interest is a dead end: just reconfigure how your skills are best used, then find another avenue within your interest that fits better. Say you want to be an actor, but you've been slinging coffee for years to pay the bills and you've never gotten a callback. You don't have to turn your back on the entertainment realm. Think bigger and broader. Maybe you're more suited to casting, editing footage, production work, PR, event planning for premieres, a corporate position at a network, and so on and so on. The possibilities are almost endless when you view your interests through a flexible lens.

Sometimes, the way you think your skills and interests will collide is not the way in which they end up working together. Richard Woolcott,* a cofounder of the action sports lifestyle brand Volcom, is a prime example of that sort of elasticity.

A surfer almost since birth, Richard was all set to go pro—until the unexpected struck: "I grew up very active in skateboarding and surfing. . . . I was building a professional surfing career, and then I had an accident my first year in college. I broke my neck right before I was going to go on the pro tour."

  www.roadtripnation.com/leader/richard-woolcott

Richard faced a devastating reality. Pro surfing was over for him. He could either abandon his interest in surfing entirely, or adapt, tinker, and develop new skills to keep himself aligned with his interest. He chose the latter, enrolled in school as a business major, worked at Quiksilver, and gained the entrepreneurial know-how needed to create one of the most prolific brands in sports history. "Everything shifted," he recalls. "I took that focus and turned toward the action sports industry. My background is really a big part of where I'm at today." Being CEO of a major action sports company was not his original vision, but Richard made adjustments along the way and stayed true to what was most important to him, while finding a way to still pay the bills.

If you've felt skeptical about our interest-based approach, we hope it's reassuring to see how people with vastly different skills have turned their interests into their livelihoods. Now you can see that the more surefire way to satisfaction is not just to develop skills for any old "career," regardless of whether that "career" interests you. Instead, your Economic Engine *can* be propelled by the things you really enjoy; you just might have to spend some time figuring out how.

Visit the Roadtrip Nation Interview Archive at **www.roadtripnation.com/ explore/interests** and select the Core Interest that intrigues you most (food, education, entrepreneurship, sports, and so on). Then select five different people who are each earning a living in different ways within that Core Interest. List them here and identify their Economic Engines:

LEADER   ECONOMIC ENGINE

It's going to take

10,

000 hours

In Malcolm Gladwell's best-selling book about human potential, *Outliers*, he discusses what it takes to become an expert. One of the prerequisites he mentions is that for most people, attainment of expert status takes about ten thousand hours. Ten. Thousand. Hours. Ten thousand hours of practice, digging deep, iterating, failing, reiterating, and learning. Yes, some people possess innate talents, but to truly become an expert, to really know and understand a process, it will take a long time. A very long time.

Putting in those kinds of hours can seem like an unfathomably daunting challenge. But think of it like training for a marathon. You don't walk out the door one day ready to run twenty-six miles. It's a process of development and growth. And often this journey will open new doors and spark new relationships, taking you in fresh and truly fulfilling directions.

So what are you willing to dedicate a significant amount of time to?

Go back to your Core Interests and Foundation mashups from "Two Turntables and a Microphone" (pages 148–149). Use the space here to start working out how you can spend your time building your Economic Engine. What skills could you develop that would increase your value within your Core Interests?

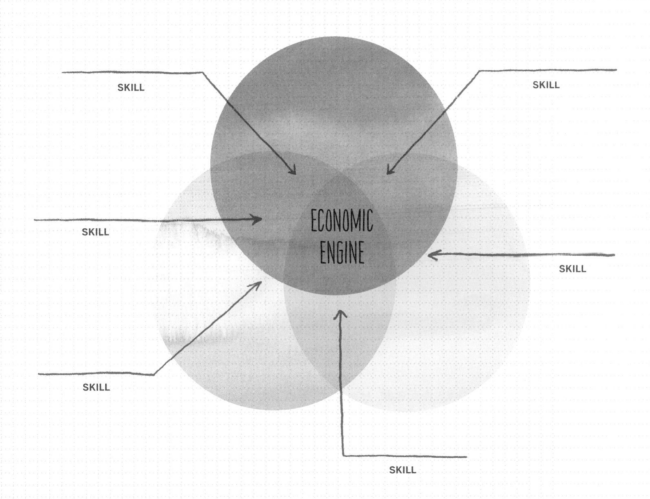

SKILL

SKILL

SKILL

SKILL

ECONOMIC ENGINE

SKILL

SKILL

CHAPTER 14

ROADMAP

The process of Self-Construction is ever-evolving and requires constant self-examination of who you are and who you want to be. It's about asking yourself tough questions and recalibrating if things aren't feeling quite right—and it entails a heck of a lot of trust that the exploration you're doing will lead you where you want to go.

When you're building your life around your interests, there are going to be times when you feel confident in your decisions, and times when doubt, fear, and anxiety leave you feeling lost again. In those dark moments, when you're frustrated and confused and aren't sure what the next step is—when your head is spinning with the question "What the hell am I doing with my life?"—it can be comforting to have something tangible to hold onto.

For us, that tangible thing was a Roadmap. So we've designed one you can try out.

This Roadmap is not a set of turn-by-turn directions. It's a framework for you to fill in and reference as you navigate your life. Only you know the nuances of your Foundation and Core Interests, and only you know how and in what ways they align with your values and vision. In other words, the only life map you'll ever need is one that you create.

Take a second and look over all the combinations of Foundation + Core Interests that you put together on pages 148–149. But this time, look at those combinations through the lens of what we've talked about since—skills, your Economic Engine, and Subjective Truths. With this new perspective, some combinations will make more sense, and others will fail to connect as well as they did when you first wrote them down. Look for the combination that you think has the best likelihood of generating a whole, unique, and fulfilling Worklife and fill that in on the following diagram.

This is your Roadmap. At least for today.

Hang your Roadmap on your wall, fold it up and keep it in your wallet, or bring it to life online. Go to www.roadtripnation.com/roadmap, punch in your Foundation and Core Interests, and find Leaders who have fashioned occupations while being guided by a Roadmap similar to yours.

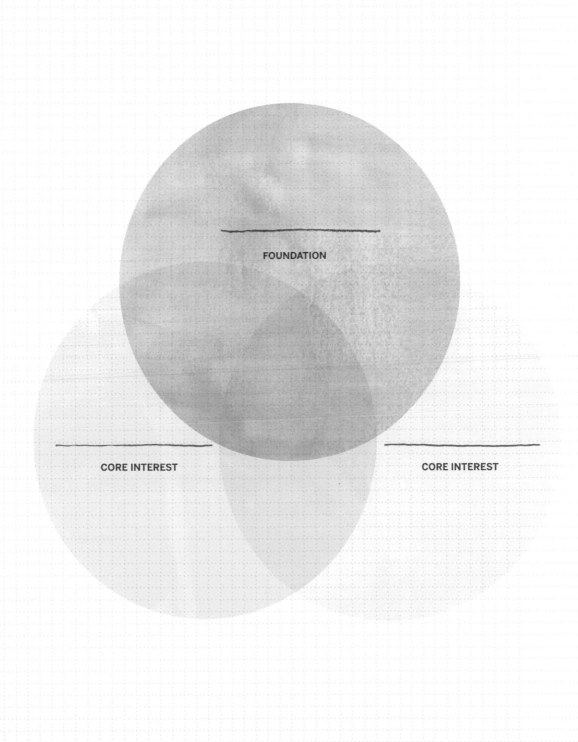

FOUNDATION

CORE INTEREST

CORE INTEREST

If the map you've created isn't working for you, or you find yourself experiencing those familiar lost feelings again, here is another Roadmap you can use to recalibrate yourself. And let's be frank: It's really only three overlapping circles. (You could do it on a napkin if you wanted to!)

Use your Roadmap as a guide. From choosing a major or part-time job, to changing careers, or even down to the simple things like choosing a magazine subscription or how to spend your free time, this framework will keep you on course.

It won't tell you exactly what your next destination will be or what next step you need to take, but it will give you comfort that the direction you are heading in is one that is most true to who you are. And if it doesn't, do it again . . . and again . . . and again.

198

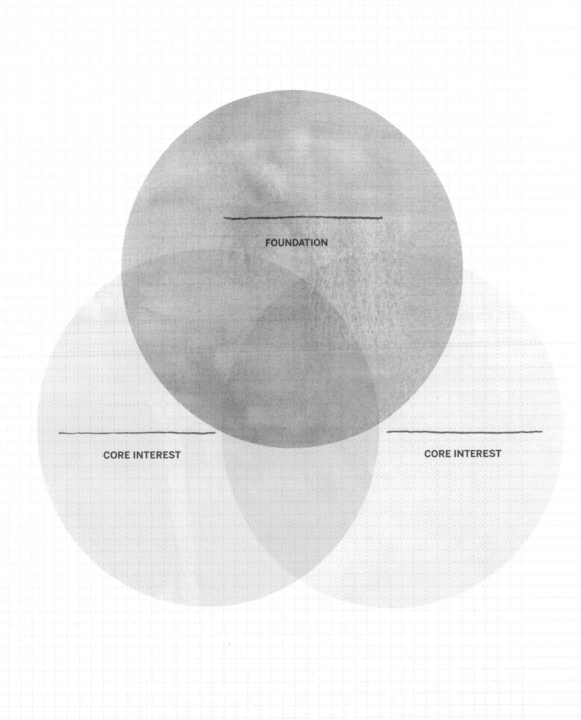

FOUNDATION

CORE INTEREST

CORE INTEREST

BEC

OME

CHAPTER 15

DRIP. DRIP. SPLASH.

Plotting out your Roadmap is a major triumph. It can make you feel like you've just climbed the Matterhorn. *Finally, direction! Satisfaction is achievable!* And trust us, it truly is. But then you start to think, "What now?" And all of a sudden, you're back at the bottom of the summit. In the face of the daunting path from who you are today to the person you want to be tomorrow, paralysis sets in.

The goal can seem so far away and impossible to achieve. Movement of any kind can be difficult to start. It's easy to get lost in debating the exact "right" next step. But what if, instead of being frozen in indecision, you simply moved?

Vicki Smith, the video game designer we mentioned earlier, summed it up this way: "I knew a priest, when I was in college and drifting, who told me that it's impossible to steer a bike that's standing still." She told us, "Just go for things. If you move forward, you'll find your way because your way will be informed by who you are. **At some point, you need to stop wondering what you are going to do with your life and just go out and do something."**

When you're guided by your Roadmap, sometimes the specifics of your decision aren't nearly as important as making a decision itself. The small choices you make today will lead to new relationships and new opportunities, all more in line with your interests and values than where you were when you began. Leap. Or hop. Or skip. Or stroll. Or even crawl. Take that as your starting point. And just move. And then move again. Every body of water, no matter how big, starts with a single drop. And then another.

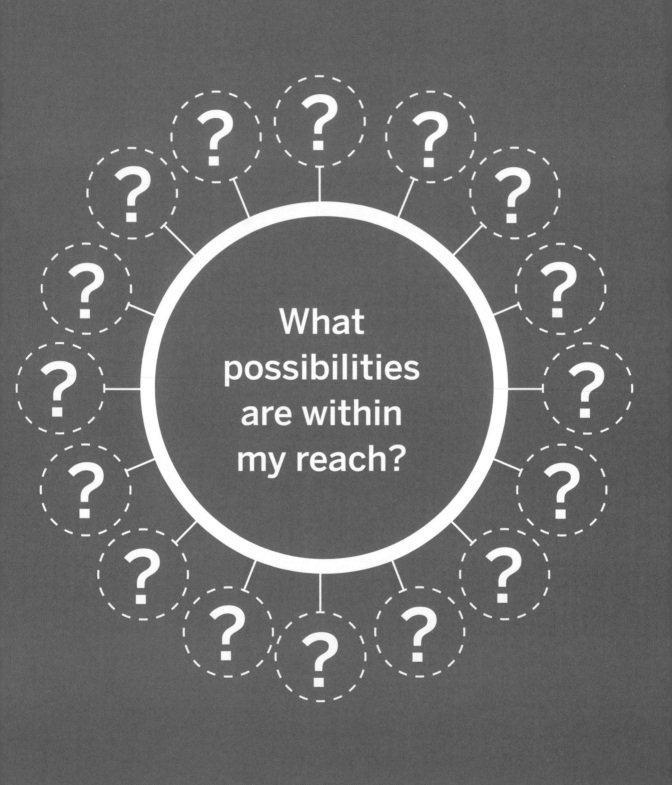

When we met with Jad Abumrad from *Radiolab* (see page 82), he introduced us to the idea of the Adjacent Possible, a powerful concept culled from the study of evolution. Jad told us, "If you imagine the primordial soup, it was full of all these chemicals; like, arsenic was in there, there's amino acids floating around. Those things aren't going to suddenly bump into each other and create a human being, you know? Or even a flower. It's not part of the possibility of that space to create the flower."

So, how did we get flowers and human beings from that stew of inhospitable chemicals?

"You can take an amino acid, and you can take a fat cell, and you can slam them together; suddenly you've got a [new] cell. And that cell has more possibilities. It can become a two-celled organism, and eventually an amoeba," Jad explained. And so it goes, on down the line of Adjacent Possibilities, until we get to people building skyscrapers and decoding genomes and writing TV show recaps.

"You have to ask yourself," Jad continued, "what is your Adjacent Possible? In some sense, right now you're in your own primordial soup of dreams. But you have to think of your possibilities in their most expansive and their most constrained [forms]. Like, okay, I can't be Michael Jordan, but maybe I could go play in a pickup game or work on my jump shot, or something like that. You have to ask yourself, what is possible right outside my border?"

In order to cultivate the virtue of humility, Benjamin Franklin said we should "imitate Jesus and Socrates." Whether or not you agree with his sentiment, the key word here is "imitate." Franklin understood that in order to succeed at something, you basically have to start out pretending to be able to do it and figure it out along the way. Franklin championed a fake-it-till-you-make-it approach for the eighteenth century: imitate what you want to be until you actually become it. If you've spent time identifying your Foundation and exploring your Core Interests, you will know roughly what you want. So start walking toward it.

You may feel a little bit like a huckster when you're in the process of faking it till you make it, but if you really go for it with intention, you'll find yourself on the way to your Roadmap. Take Jakob Laggner,* the cofounder of Treks and Tracks, a firm that leads outdoor education courses. An immigrant from Austria to America, Jakob was working in a call center and bored out of his mind. During his downtime at the office, he started building a website for his dream company.

Describing the services of his not-yet-formed business, Jakob listed skiing, rock climbing, trips to New Zealand, and other expeditions he and his friends had undertaken. He listed his site on a community website called Bay Area Kid Fun, and suddenly started getting sign-ups for his excursions. He remembers thinking, "Oh my God! I don't have insurance. I don't have a permit. I just made this up." But that forced him to enlist a buddy who had experience with camps, and together they made it happen. Cut to now, years later: leading out-door tours and climbing adventures for Treks and Tracks is Jakob's full-time job—just like what he had proposed in his "fake" business.

  www.roadtripnation.com/leader/jakob-laggner

HOW TO GET TO MARS IN TEN MILLION TINY STEPS OR LESS

Adam Steltzner,* the lead mechanical engineer of NASA's Mars *Curiosity* rover landing, is not entirely sure that he graduated from high school. Did he ever get that pesky C-minus in a long-forgotten class that was required for his diploma? He's never gone back and checked. At that time, grades weren't really important to Adam, but if you trace his path, you see strong evidence of the Adjacent Possible, of the deep power of tiny actions to move a life in unexpected and exciting ways.

Looking back at Adam's post–high school life, NASA didn't really seem like it was on his list of targets. Adam worked as a cashier at a health food store, and played bass in a string of rock bands. He had the directionless quality that so many of us feel when we're off the path of our Roadmap. But then late one night, while driving home after playing a show, he looked up at the sky.

"I started to notice that when I would return home from playing a show at night, the stars were in a different place in the sky," Adam recalled. "I was thinking, 'Whoa. They're moving. Why do they move?' Obviously, I really wasn't paying attention in high school. . . . And so I literally went to the local community college to take an astronomy course to teach me why the stars were moving."

 www.roadtripnation.com/leader/adam-steltzner

One class at a community college. One small, simple step.

DRIP

"Then they had a conceptual physics course, so it was physics without the math," Adam recalls.

+

DRIP

It turned out Adam loved physics.

=

SPLASH

Today, Adam Steltzner is directing spacecraft landings on planets millions of miles away. Can you imagine telling that to the twentysomething Adam who didn't even understand basic planetary systems? It would've seemed like an ocean of drips away.

The best part about taking the small steps is that it prepares you for the big ones. Everything is fractal; you're just doing the same thing on a bigger scale—following simple steps that make it easier to face the fear and the setbacks. Take Adam's thoughts on the distinct possibility that the (very expensive) *Curiosity* might not have survived its touchdown on the red planet. "If we had put a smoking hole on the surface of Mars," he reflects, "I would have definitely failed. But I think humanity is better for trying that and making a smoking hole on the surface of Mars than [for] never having tried."

"I had to surrender to the act
of doing, rather than the promise
of success or something at the
end of it. Surrender to the process,
rather than the goal."

—**ADAM STELTZNER**, *mechanical engineer, NASA*

Look back at your Roadmap. Think about the first tiny steps that you can take to align with your Foundation and Core Interests. List things that will take no more than ten minutes, such as reading a blog, subscribing to a magazine, or following someone on Twitter whose work aligns with one of your Core Interests. Then ramp it up a little bit. List things that will take a bit more time. Try visiting a museum, attending a Meetup gathering, signing up for a class, or taking a Skillshare. Keep ramping it up until you have a page full of first steps.

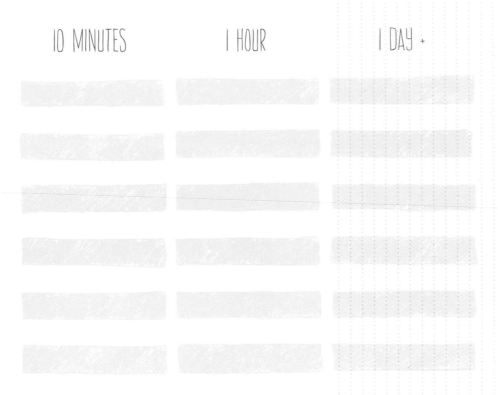

10 MINUTES   1 HOUR   1 DAY +

The Projects at the end of this book will help you, too. We've given you a general framework for each of them, as well as an idea about the level of engagement it will take to get started.

The cumulative effect of action is
the most powerful force in defining
your road.

Do something.

Then do something else.

Then do something else.

Then splash.

Put this book down for the next ten minutes and take one of the actions you just
listed. Make your first move. It may seem like just a small drip, but that's okay!

CHAPTER 16

YOU ARE YOUR DECISIONS

Do you want the spiritual explanation or the scientific one? Thankfully, this is an instance when they both agree: you aren't what you feel, you aren't what you say, you are what you *do*. From the Bhagavad Gita to the Bible, cheesy motivational speakers to Jean-Paul Sartre, society at large emphasizes the importance of your actions in shaping who you are. Even in science, ideas like neuroplasticity show how the pathways in our brain are restructured by our everyday decisions. No matter how you parse it out, it's pretty simple: You are the sum of your actions.

If you wake up Monday morning, go to a job you hate all day, and then go home and watch TV all night, then that's exactly who you are: a person who hates his job and watches TV all night. If, on the other hand, you are a person who hates her job, but you're also taking night classes to help you make an eventual Worklife transition, and you spend time organizing a weekly mountain biking expedition with your friends, that is a decidedly different identity, one built on the power of your own actions, no matter how small.

Imagine buying a TV, hooking it up to cable, turning it on to whatever station it happens to be set to, and then just sitting down and never changing the channel. That's unintentional living; that's life on the Assembly Line. If we simply live the life that's put in front of us—if we just watch "what's on" and never change the channel, we'll be subjected to a lot of garbage; we'll be dissatisfied, bored, frustrated, and, worst of all, entirely ignorant of what else we could be "watching."

Perhaps, stuck there on that metaphorical couch, we'll find ourselves saying, "Tomorrow." Or "Next weekend." Or "Next month." Or "Next semester." We're all familiar with how this plays out: Tomorrow I'll do that Photoshop tutorial, but tonight I'm going to binge-watch an entire season of that new zombie meth-lab biker-gang comedy on Netflix. Next semester I'll enroll in that ecology class I've been vowing to take for the last six years. Next weekend I really will write a blog instead of watching YouTube videos of pandas sneezing. You can continue to delay, but just remember, there is no aspirational "you" waiting around the corner. **What you do today is who you are.**

The words "choose" and "decide" are everything. Our day is filled with actions by which we tell ourselves (and the world) who we're choosing to be. But we tend to think of our everyday decisions as weightless, rather than imbuing them with the power they deserve.

Whom should I hang out with? What do I do with my free time? The answer to any one of the thousand questions we run through each day is just that—an answer to a single question. But what do all those answers add up to? Me. You. Us. We are our decisions. Our lives are the accumulation of everything we choose to do. And what we choose not to do. **Intention is the key.**

We all have moments in our lives that we consider milestones. Events or accomplishments that help define who we are—landing a killer job, getting a degree, going on a life-changing journey. Big or small, these milestones hold a secret that we can learn from.

That secret is, quite simply, their history. What were the decisions that, when added up, created that milestone? What led Sonia Sotomayor from the Bronx to Princeton to a seat on the Supreme Court? What trickle-down of simple events led Stephen Hawking from a modest upbringing in London to Oxford and Cambridge and then to write *A Brief History of Time*? Our achievements are birthed in the tiniest moments.

If you start tracking your decisions backward, what small decisions do you see on the path to the big milestone? Choose an accomplishment in your life and write out the chain of actions that led you to it.

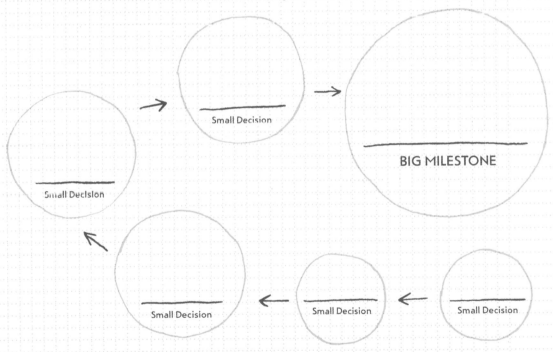

Small Decision

BIG MILESTONE

Small Decision

Small Decision

Small Decision

Small Decision

Now that you've thought about the small decisions in your past, start considering the present. What milestones will emerge for you? What small decisions are you making right now that will lead you to the next version of yourself? **What decisions are you not making that you should be?**

Decision

No decision

Making no
decision

Surrendering control to the Assembly Line

That is the essence behind "Drip. Drip. Splash." Any movement is better than no movement, certainly, but it's even better when intention is the driving force. A common example of this pops up all the time when you (or your friends) are going through your mid-to-late-twenties "What the hell am I doing with my life?" freak-outs. Suddenly it seems like everybody you know is going back to school for an MBA, or a law degree, or a teaching certificate. You may be one of those very people. Some of those people going back to school may have a clear sense of why this is an important step for them, but for many others, that choice is more of a reaction to the dissatisfaction of where they are than a step in the direction of what they want.

Acting haphazardly out of aimless desperation often leads to magnified discontent. You finally took action and put in the work (and potentially a lot of money), yet you're still adrift, just on a slightly modified Assembly Line.

220

That's exactly what happened to Liz Mandarano,* the owner and instructor of a New York City yoga studio. After graduating from college, Liz bobbed along the Assembly Line. "I did what a lot of people do—I thought, I'll just go to graduate school. I ended up picking law school. I was too immature. I didn't even think about the repercussions of the loans, or whether I wanted to be a lawyer. Or what being a lawyer was like. I thought about dropping out after a year, but I'm not a quitter, and my ego got in the way, and I kept accumulating debt."

Liz worked as a lawyer for seven unhappy years. Basically, the sum of Liz's decisions had not led her to a version of herself that was satisfying. And then Liz took a small, simple action. Admiring the outward and inward peace of a colleague, she followed her coworker's lead and started taking yoga classes.

* **www.roadtripnation.com/leader/liz-mandarano**

What followed for Liz was a journey forged from a single decision. She started doing yoga once a week, then six months later, it was twice a week, then three times a week, then four. "I really felt peaceful," she recalls. As she became more engaged by her lifestyle changes, she knew that working at an unsatisfying job couldn't continue. She'd reached work-life balance, but what she craved was Worklife integration. "I was at dinner with two of my friends and I was chatting about this concept that I had, and one of them just looked at me and said, 'You should open a yoga studio.' That was in May 2005, and this place was open September of 2005; it was as if the second she said it, I had to do it."

It's not always an instant process, and we shouldn't expect overnight results. But when you're in the mire, when you're confused, when you're uninspired, ask questions about the choices you are and are not making. Are you acting based on how something will look on Facebook, or to give your parents bragging rights around the holiday table? Are you laying the bricks of a road you hate because you made unintentional choices, like Liz did? There's always room to make new intentional choices. Coasting should never be an option.

Remember Van Taylor Monroe, the shoe artist from a few chapters back? Before he was able to support himself with his art, Van made a daily decision that shaped him into the next version of himself. Every day, he painted. This meant that he wasn't just a guy working in a finance job he hated; he was that *plus* he was an artist. He made the choice to stay up late painting because he loved it, and a shoe Van painted in his spare time was directly responsible for his present-day lifestyle. **Again, work-life balance transforms into an integrated Worklife through a steady stream of choices.**

221

Van told us, "Anybody who was around me probably knew, 'Okay, every time I see Van, he's painting tennis shoes or he's painting something, he's going to do something with painting.' Whatever your dream is, if I follow you around for a week, I should know what it is without you telling me."

If you'd been followed around by a hidden camera crew last week, would the footage of those seven days tell a story that reflects who you want to be? Do your habits flow out of your Roadmap, or are they the result of the Assembly Line?

At the moment of decision making, there's a little bit of knee-jerk reaction that stops us. Your job is to resist that, no matter how difficult it might be. **You have to resist the knee-jerk response in order to reach the next version of yourself.**

In college, Ariel Helwani* wanted to be a journalist for the mixed martial arts community. Two problems: he had no experience, and he was incredibly shy. "I used to sit in my dorm my freshman year," Ariel recalls, "and I would wait until 2:30 A.M. to make sure everybody was asleep just to go brush my teeth and run back to my room."

That shyness should've kept Ariel away from broadcasting, but eventually his drive to be involved in MMA superseded his anxiety and he dove in. He started hosting a radio show about wrestling and the mixed martial arts community called the *Main Event*. He'd meekly walk to the broadcasting booth, head down, but he came alive in the studio.

Ariel kept building on that first action. He engaged with professional fighters every day. His persistence and professional approach eventually landed him interviews and helped him develop a popular blog, which got him a job at a website that covered MMA, which then turned into an offer from AOL to get paid

  www.roadtripnation.com/leader/ariel-helwani

for what he'd been doing for free. "Just *live* the dream," Ariel told us. "There's no reason that any one of us can't do what we love doing."

Kansas City, Missouri–based letterpress artist Michelle Dreher talked to us about the dangers of delaying action, of waiting for the *right time*: "When I decided to start my own shop, I had no idea exactly what was going to happen, but it was better than waiting for the right moment. . . . Time passes so fast. You're just sitting there, thinking about 'What do I want to do?' and then it's five years later."

Waiting for your proverbial ducks to be in a row, your bank account to be at just the right level, or your experience to be exactly where you want it to be is a common practice, but living this way is a version of the deferred-life plan. **You're never going to be totally comfortable starting something. Stop waiting for the right time.**

"You're always going to feel a sense of hesitation either way," says Marshawn Evans, an attorney and the president of Chicago's Communication Counts, a public speaking and personal branding firm. "Don't let one choice weigh you down so much that it's hard for you to hear yourself."

Commitment is the antidote to paralysis-by-analysis.

If you're feeling paralyzed by the choices in front of you, return to your Roadmap. If the choice you want to make is taking you one step closer to the center of your Roadmap, then you're going in the right direction.

And what if you're wrong? So what? Think of it not as a mistake, but rather trial and error. Actions that don't pan out will show you which path is yours and which path isn't, leading you to the next, better beta version of yourself.

Think back to that invisible documentary film crew following you around for a week. Do the contents of your days match your vision of who you are and who you see as your future self? Are they putting you on your Roadmap? Are you proud of your actions?

Earlier, we broke down the number of hours worked in an average lifetime (about 90,000). During every twenty-four hours, you've got another eight hours or so outside of work in which you have to eat, commute, get dressed, shower (not necessarily in that order!), and do all the other chores of daily life. What's left is the time you have to invest in yourself. So exactly how do you use your time?

Let's lay it out with a little math.

1 **Things You Have to Do (in hours)** → **2**

_____ Time at work

_____ Commuting

_____ Eating

_____ Sleeping

_____ Grooming (teeth, showers, dressing, and all that)

+ _____ Errands and other responsibilities
_____

_____ **Total Have-to-Do's**

24 Hours in a day

− _____ Have-to-Do's (your answer to #1)
_____

_____ **Total free time per day**

Now that you have your average day figured out, think about how you used your free time last week.

MONDAY	TUESDAY	WEDNESDAY	THURSDAY

FRIDAY	SATURDAY	SUNDAY

How do you feel looking at the week above? Are you using your time with intention? What small decisions are you making to set the stage for the next version of yourself? Are you moving closer to the core of your Roadmap—to that place where your Core Interests and Foundation converge? (Good news: You can count the time you've spent reading this book as getting you closer.)

SO, WHAT WILL YOU DO WITH TOMORROW'S FREE TIME?
AND THE NEXT DAY'S?
AND THE DAY AFTER THAT?

COMFORT IS OVERRATED

That's right: Comfort *is* overrated. That's a bold statement in today's world, but we mean it. In the face of stress, failure, and hardship, we follow a natural impulse—we crave the cocoon. But when comfort acts as a barrier to intentional living, it can become a doorway to regret, boredom, and disillusionment.

One of our Roadtrippers, Zachariah Cowan, struggled with the allure of comfort in the face of defining his own road. During his Roadtrip, he told us, "One of my favorite quotes is, 'The greatest nemesis to change is the conflict between what you want to become and how you want to feel.' I really want to feel good all the time, and that has really been degrading my growth. It has been degrading my life, it has been degrading everything I'm trying to accomplish."

That human desire to feel good right now, to chomp the proverbial candy bar in the face of stress and uncertainty, only leads to a string of ineffectual Band-Aids.

This is basic do-your-homework, do-your-chores kind of stuff. Do the hard work first, and then the candy bar isn't a Band-Aid, it's a pleasant pit stop on your Roadmap. Don't shy away from the hard work.

Say, for instance, you want to make it in TV production. What do you do? Christian Jacobs,* lead singer of the Aquabats and cocreator of the screwball children's TV sensation *Yo Gabba Gabba*, advises, "Make things tough for yourself." It's a strange concept coming from such an exuberant personality, a guy who seems to base his whole life on play and toys (his office is crammed with robots and monsters of all stripes), but to Christian, play and work are one and the same.

  www.roadtripnation.com/leader/christian-jacobs

They are fully integrated. "Attitude is your altitude," he tells us. "Successful people all have that positive attitude, 'I'm gonna go for it, and if I lose I lose, but I'm going for it!'

"You've gotta throw yourself in the frying pan," he urged. Go in big and stay big, no matter what. And don't skimp.

"Work at a production company and learn the ropes, but be ambitious. **Don't just go home and watch _Lost_ after work; stay up late and write a script.**"

Decision making is tough, scary work. It's the heavy-lifting, sweaty grunt work of Self-Construction. It's where we define ourselves. Our actions are a chisel with which we sculpt our identity. So ask yourself: Who are you? Better yet: whom do you _want_ to be?

227

CHAPTER 17

HUSTLE

There is no one way to define your own road in life. This reminds us of the phrase "There's more than one way to skin a cat." (Yes, the visual here is gross, and to be clear for the PETA folks, we're not at all endorsing the actual act . . . but stay with us—the analogy really works.) The point here is that, as the phrase implies, defining your own road takes creativity and determination and there's a million different ways to do it. But no matter what road you take there will always be times when you will have to grin, bear it, and slog through some seriously thankless tasks. No matter what or how you do it, you're just going to have to get down and do the dirty work. **This place where creativity meets hard work is what we call the hustle.**

Hustle is about relentlessly pursuing the skills and experience you need to grow. It means not stopping. It's working for free to get your foot in the door. It's taking on the shit work and doing it well. It's chipping away at the wall until you make a hole big enough to slip through (*Shawshank Redemption*–style) and make your presence known on the other side. It's making it to the finish line, regardless of failures and setbacks. It's believing that what you have to offer is worth fighting for.

Hustle is all about, as author and Nike branding guru Kevin Carroll* told us, "putting your dream out on the street."

  www.roadtripnation.com/leader/kevin-carroll

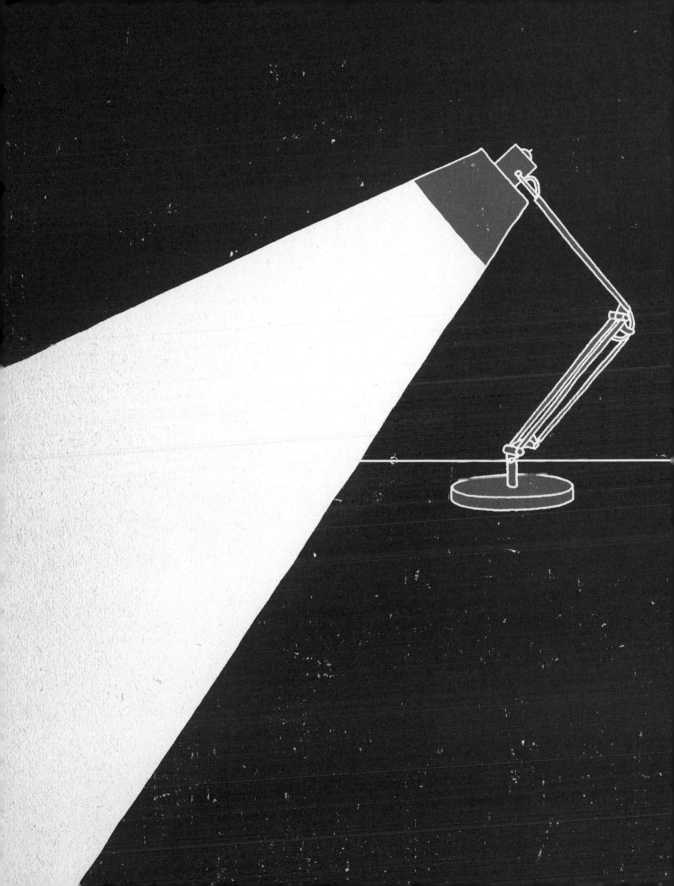

"You have to be willing to put your dream on the street."

—**KEVIN CARROLL**, *the Katalyst, Nike*

Kevin's hustle started on the basketball court. "Little did I know that this ball was actually taking me on a journey," Kevin told us, holding a basketball in his hands. "This ball gave me courage, taught me how to deal with disappointment, taught me how to deal with things beyond my life." Kevin's potential pro career was destroyed when he blew out his knee, but this setback didn't stop his hustle.

Kevin realigned his Roadmap, studying sports medicine. He become a trainer for high school and college teams, and then later had a seven-year run as "the Katalyst" at Nike, with a mandate to bring about creative change in the company. Along the way, he also wrote a great book, *Rules of the Red Rubber Ball*.

"People told me that bouncing this ball would get me nowhere in life," Kevin recalled. "Those were the same people who asked me for tickets when I was the head trainer for the Philadelphia 76ers." Kevin was intentional about his choices and did the hard work because, for him, it was fun—it is what he loves to do— and that sense of joy motivated him to keep hustling. "When you're out there playing, you start to imagine yourself as something bigger than you are. That's how I've always done it. I see my dream in action."

Hustling is what makes the improbable the inevitable.

Your Vision

HUS

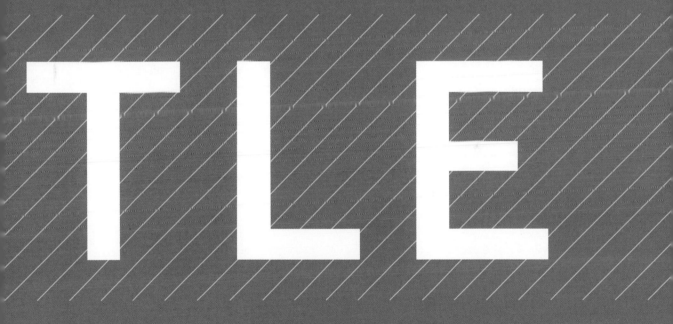

TLE

Your Open Road

Don't wait for an invitation to start living your life. You can hustle up the traditional corporate ladder, but these days there's just as much opportunity to hustle by inventing your own ladder. Create these opportunities instead of reacting to circumstance, even if it makes you feel foolish, even if it seems impossible.

Just about every new generation gets criticized for its perceived sense of entitlement. Today it's unapologetic interns showing up late to their posts, carrying an iced coffee in one hand and texting with the other, quitting early in the day and still expecting that promotion to creative director. Whether this is a true portrayal is hard to say, but one thing is true for sure: building an inspired Worklife is not a gift that falls into your lap; it has to be earned—especially if you want to keep it. Success is the payoff for effort, so get used to the effort. And if you can, find a way to enjoy it.

"It's like when you're in sports, and all you want to do is play," says Vicki Smith, the video game designer you met in "Life Is Only Linear in the Rearview Mirror." "If you don't do the push-ups, you don't get to play the game." For Vicki, the conditioning she had to do before being able to design games came in the form of learning more math and science. No matter what you want to do, there will be some form of conditioning you'll have to suffer through to get in shape enough to do it. Not only will it not be easy, you shouldn't want it to be easy. Relishing the shit work—or at least keeping a positive and intentional attitude about it—is a standout quality that will elevate you over those who won't, or can't, or who half-ass it, and it will develop your endurance and problem-solving skills.

"Think of your situation like a tripod, and each of those legs has a name. One of them is luck, the other one is talent (meaning ability), and the other is hard work. Although one of those things will get you into a situation, you have to get another one of those legs on the ground as quickly as possible. Because the world is full of people who are talented, who were not lucky and did not work hard, who kind of washed out. Recognize that any one of those things will get you into a situation. Your job is to get two of them connected as soon as you can and hope for the day when you get all three connected."

—**WALTER MURCH**, *film editor/sound designer of* Apocalypse Now

Naturally, shit work will still feel shitty when you're in the midst of whatever menial task you're pushing through, but when it's in the service of your Roadmap, it's still a million times better than life on the Assembly Line. So when you find yourself knee-deep in a pile of shit work, printing a 300-page report on a printer that jams every five minutes, remind yourself that getting through it is a key part of the hustle, an intentional act in the process of Self-Construction, so silence the part of your brain that thinks you're above it.

BE HUMBLE AND SACRIFICE

"I slept in my car at every rest stop along the New Jersey Turnpike," says Wendy Williams,* now a successful TV and radio personality, as she recalls weekends spent working at a radio station in New York City while she juggled a full-time job in Washington, DC, where she lived. Wendy worked a low-paying entry-level job in radio. "I had a comforter, an alarm clock, and a pillow in the back. I put my seat on recline. I had a portable toothbrush. I would take a bird bath in the bathroom, and I'd show up at the radio station and do my shift. That's the way I did it."

In the midst of the hustle, your sacrifice might not be financial—it could be doing a job that seems demeaning or beneath you, all in pursuit of the greater goal. Morris Reid,* a government lobbyist, had already run an Ohio field office for President Bill Clinton's campaign when he got a call from Hillary Clinton's office. "I packed everything I had and jumped on a Greyhound bus," Morris recalls. But when he got there, he revealed to a friend at Hillary's office that his real goal was to work for his idol, Secretary of Commerce Ron Brown. He asked, he hustled, a trusted colleague made some calls, and Morris was called in by Ron Brown's assistant.

*  www.roadtripnation.com/leader/wendy-williams

* 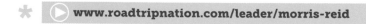 www.roadtripnation.com/leader/morris-reid

"There are a million ways to get to success; for me, it wasn't about who I knew, it was about the hustle."

—**WENDY WILLIAMS**, *TV and radio host*

"I get there," Morris says, "and he says, 'I got something for you. Your job is to take care of Ron Brown's mother and mother-in-law.' I was on 'purse duty' with a couple of old ladies!" Morris took happy ownership of what could've been viewed as babysitting detail: getting them to places, helping them along. Morris's aplomb made him a favorite with the two women. "They talked about me nonstop," he laughs. After demonstrating his commitment through hard work and positive energy, his goodwill (and the mothers chatting him up to Secretary Brown) moved him up to exactly where he wanted to be, as Brown's protégé.

JUST SAY YES

The James Beard Award–winning pastry chef and Food Network host Gale Gand* related a story to us about the time she got the opportunity that launched her as a professional baker. Early in her career, Gale got a call from a previous boss who had a pastry position available. Gale had only worked a couple of kitchen jobs; pastries were not yet in her repertoire.

"I thought, am I the person who says 'Sure, yeah,' or do I throw up obstacles and say 'Oh, I'm not quite ready?'" Gale said yes, and there she was, a pastry chef. When faced with learning a new field, Gale advises, "You need to lie and say you're qualified, and then when you get there, you will be. One day in passing, this chef says to me, 'Do you know how to make croissants?' And the right answer to everything in the kitchen is 'Yes, chef.' So what do I do? After work, I make seven different batches of croissants from seven different books. I stay up all night, teach myself how to do it. So the next day, when the chef asks me the same question, I'm not lying." The takeaway? Just say yes.

  www.roadtripnation.com/leader/gale-gand

Another key insight into Gale's hustle was actually something she learned from legendary chef and hustler, Julia Child: learn how to sell yourself. When Gale had revealed that she taught herself instead of going to culinary school, Julia exclaimed, "Oh, darling, never say you're self-taught. Always say you learned in the field!"

THERE'S ALWAYS ANOTHER WAY IN

Sometimes you have to find a different way into the house. When we were planning our first Roadtrip, we fudged the truth a bit to get into a particularly intimidating house: the, ahem—cough, cough—highest court in the nation.

We wanted to interview U.S. Supreme Court Justice Sandra Day O'Connor—the first woman on the Supreme Court, and a cowgirl at heart, who had ruled on some of the most important cases in recent history. We had to hear her story.

"I looked everywhere for phone numbers to the Supreme Court, and all I could find was a random number for booking tours on its website," remembers Nathan, one of the original Roadtrippers. "I called up and asked for Sandra. 'You mean Justice O'Connor?' the guy on the line corrected me. 'Uh, yeah, Justice Sandra Day O'Connor,' I answered."

The guy at the tour office told Nathan that directly speaking to O'Connor was out of the question. "You can come take a tour if you want, or you can write a letter to Justice O'Connor." Nathan wrote the letter, waited a few weeks, and called back.

He got the same guy, who was unaffected by Nathan's frustration over not hearing from Justice O'Connor. "I don't know what to tell you," he said. "You can come take a tour if you want, or you can write another letter."

Nathan kept writing letters, kept calling, kept getting the same response month after month. Finally, Nathan tried a bold (crazy?) move. "This was in the days before caller ID. I called up the tour number one last time, but I used a deep, stern, business-guy voice. 'Sir!' I said testily, 'I was just speaking with Justice O'Connor and was transferred here. Please transfer me back right away!'

"Meanwhile, my mom was downstairs making lunch, while I was sweating through my shirt, thinking NSA agents just might bust through the door. But my creative approach worked. The official stammered out an apology and transferred me over to Justice O'Connor's office."

Justice O'Connor's assistant graciously listened to Nate's frazzled story about the Green RV and the Roadtrippers' mission. A month later, the assistant called back to say that Justice O'Connor would meet with them.

The point here isn't to lie to Supreme Court justices (or anyone else, for that matter). The point is to get creative. It's often said that the definition of an insane person is someone who keeps doing the same action but expects a different result. If what you're doing isn't working, try a new approach; there's always a way in.

PUT YOURSELF IN PROXIMITY

When you get down to it, this is the overarching goal of all the decisions on your Roadmap—to get you within striking distance of what you want. Beth McCarthy-Miller,* a director for *Saturday Night Live* and *30 Rock* and an eight-time director of the MTV Video Music Awards, says she didn't walk into SNL and start directing right away. In fact, Beth started her career as an intern at CNN's Washington bureau, where she did *everything*. She remembers, "I ran the prompter, I did camera, I ran cable."

From CNN, Beth took the skills she had accumulated and leapt to MTV, which put her closer to her goal of working in entertainment. But it wasn't an upward leap. She began a low-paying internship at the network, staying afloat by waiting tables and working at Gap. Beth says, "I worked my butt off for a long time. I was working a lot of hours and making no money. Not every experience is going to have you saying 'Wow, I'm so glad I'm doing this,' but it might open up the doors to something else." It didn't matter how trivial her tasks at MTV were; she was gaining experience and developing skills in the world she wanted to be a part of.

* ▶ **www.roadtripnation.com/leader/beth-mccarthy-miller**

WORK HARDER

That's hustle in a nutshell. Ahmir "Questlove" Thompson, drummer of The Roots, told us about his personal drive: "Average day, I do eighteen-, twenty-hour days. It's a constant mission to stay ahead."

CNN anchor Soledad O'Brien said to us, "The really good stories are not the ones where eighteen satellite trucks are parked. They're the ones where you drive a little extra distance, you ask the little extra questions, you dig a little bit harder." This vision of journalism is a reflection of the hard work Soledad has put in. "I worked my way up. I was a production assistant, went on to become a writer trainee, then went to NBC, and then I got a job at the NBC affiliate in San Francisco, where I made about a third of what everybody else made. I was a terrible reporter, no experience. But I knew I could outwork people. I might have had no clue about what I'd been assigned to do, but I knew that I would outwork everybody, and I would stay until midnight if I had to figure it out."

Every one of the stories in this chapter underscores that there are two kinds of hard work: There's hamster-like hard work, running furiously in a plastic wheel that spins and spins and goes nowhere, and there's beaver-style hard work, damming a river to suit your needs, working step by step toward an appreciable goal.

Hustle without a Roadmap is just busywork. But when your hustle is working hand in hand with your Roadmap—when it's connected to your authentic Core Interests and speaks to your Foundation—that's when the hustle can be energizing and powerful. That's when it will get your dream on the street.

WHAT DOES YOUR HUSTLE LOOK LIKE?

WHAT DO I NEED TO **SAY YES** TO?

_____

WHAT **SIDE DOOR** HAVE I NOT
OPENED THAT I SHOULD?

_____

_____

_____

WHAT IS WITHIN MY **REACH**?

_____

WHAT DO I NEED TO **SACRIFICE**?

_____

WHAT **SHIT WORK** DO I HAVE TO DO
TO GET WHERE I WANT TO BE?

_____

WHAT **BASIC RESOURCE** AM I NOT USING?

_____

CHAPTER 18

RISK OR REGRET? YOU CHOOSE.

Taking risks leads to **danger**.

Taking risks leads to **rewards**.

Each of these statements is true. You just need to balance the two as you move toward the center of your Roadmap. Your job is to intentionally approach risk and determine what's at the heart of the risky decision you're considering. What are the long-term consequences of not taking a particular risk? What are the short-term dangers? What can you gain? What can you lose?

At first, you'll probably end up no less confused after this examination. And that's mainly because the whole point of taking a risk is that you don't know what's going to happen. That's why it seems risky. (And by the way, we're all grown-ups here, and we don't have to formally define what we mean by "risk," right? We don't mean dumb decisions. We mean decisions that don't have a certain, predictable outcome but do have the potential to shape your road in unexpected ways, good or otherwise.)

In facing risk, it's necessary to remind ourselves that we are the sum of our decisions. Is taking the risk going to keep us on our Roadmap, even if we might fail and there might be consequences we didn't foresee? Will the regret in not taking a risk pile up like compound interest on an overdue loan, so that years from now, we are buried in "What ifs"?

"My first jump, I was terrified. And after eleven thousand jumps, there's still fear. But there's fear and fear management, and you have to weigh the rewards. I can either be too afraid to do this, and never have this amazing experience of falling 120 mph and looking at the world from 5,000 feet, because I let my fear hold me down. Look what I get for giving it a try. Look at the reward I get. Courage is not being fearless, it's acting in the face of fear. You act in the face of it, and do it anyway, because the reward is so great."

—**WARD HESSIG**, *sky-diving instructor*

As we've seen earlier, that accumulation of "What ifs" is what awaits us on the other side of the Assembly Line. The comfort of not taking a risk, of making a safe bet or "right" choice, tends to come back and bite us down the line. Cheryl Foster, the artist we met in "Defining Your Foundation," spent two decades in that comfort zone, working as a real estate appraiser, building up a heavy load of regret and dissatisfaction. Looking back on her twenty years of unsatisfying work, Cheryl admits she regretted taking the safe path.

And then Cheryl's mother was diagnosed with terminal cancer just as she was preparing to retire from a nearly thirty-year career as a schoolteacher. The reality of the deferred-life plan hit Cheryl's mom hard. "As I was administering morphine," Cheryl recalled, "she was babbling out of her mind [that] she wanted to go up in a hot-air balloon," Cheryl recalled. "She wanted to go to the Bahamas! Why wasn't there any time for that when she could still make that journey?" In that moment, Cheryl got a rare glimpse into her future. She could practically hear herself on her own deathbed wishing she'd done things differently and not squandered all her time working in real estate—something she never had any affinity for. "When she passed, that was it! I never appraised another thing," Cheryl reflects.

By the time we sat down with Cheryl she was happily doing what she loves as a multimedia artist and serving as the master artist-in-residence for the John F. Kennedy Center for the Performing Arts. It's safe to say that her experience with her mother's passing shifted her view of risk. "You wanna take the safe path? There's no joy in that. I don't want a safety net, I just want to be out there and doing it. But my happiness is a little bit different from everybody else's."

And that's a key point. When you define happiness for yourself it usually looks different from the one-size-fits-all model that society hands us. And chances are, you'll have to be willing to take the risk to pursue your definition of happiness. Because on the other side of risk lies a life that is worth living.

If you never take a risk, you never get the reward. Simple as that.

Jonathan Poneman,* the cofounder of Sub Pop Records, home of the Shins and, in the early days, Nirvana, deals with the risk/reward ratio by redefining what the terms mean.

"If everything in life is characterized as risk versus safety, the human instinct is to choose safety. But if you use a whole different standard for evaluating your life, like necessary versus unnecessary, happiness is necessary and love is necessary. For me, it was just changing the way I evaluate my life, and taking the whole idea of security out of the equation."

Let's ramp up this philosophy to a life-or-death situation. Picture, back in the day, a hypothetical caveman who wanted to feed his family. Stomachs were grumbling, and those nuts and seeds were only going to go so far. So the caveman took his spear and went out to track down a mastodon. Good eatin', those guys, if you don't get stomped, gored, or otherwise obliterated by the beast. For the caveman, spear in hand, the necessity of eating outweighs the risk of getting gored to death.

  www.roadtripnation.com/leader/jonathan-poneman

If you consider living a life that you find meaningful and engaging as a necessary act of survival, then risk, in a traditional sense, goes out the window. Like Jonathan, you will have created a new set of standards by which to judge your decisions.

NECESSARY vs UNNECESSARY

Think about some of the risks you think you should take but haven't. Use this new set of standards to decide whether the "risky" decision is one that is necessary or unnecessary to your well-being.

RISK	NECESSARY	UNNECESSARY

In the early years of Roadtrip, we were looking for an outlet to share all the stories we were collecting on the road. Our goal was to reach as many people as possible, and television seemed like the best way to do that. So, with substantial effort, we were fortunate enough to get a top-tier talent agency to help us pitch our show. We met with heads of programming at all the major networks, including the president of MTV. Interest in the show was piqued, and the idea of finally being able to pay off our debts and get some exposure for Roadtrip Nation was enticing.

The problem was, everyone wanted to warp Roadtrip Nation into Hollywood fluff. We were asked, "Can we vote someone off the RV?" and "What about driving the RV off a cliff at the end of the show?" If we had continued down this path, we'd have been able to cash a big up-front check, but it would come at the cost of sacrificing everything that mattered to us.

Still, it was tempting. We were probably $40,000 in debt at the time. But as badly as we wanted to climb out from under the interest charges building on our five or six credit card balances, we felt we couldn't cheapen the vision we had for Roadtrip Nation.

What we saw developing was a growing movement, not some get-rich-quick scheme. So we took a huge risk. We passed on all that opportunity, said no thanks to the Hollywood folks, and moved on to public television. In case you don't know, the "public" in public television is code for "no funding." We knew there would be no production funds available at the outset, but we were attracted by the mission-based programming, the longevity that most programs had, and the producers' ownership of the content. Over time we found a way to relicense that content and bring on funders who believed in our mission, and we learned how to innovate in lots of different ways to fuel the movement.

Looking back on that key inflection point in Roadtrip Nation's history, we don't know if we'd be around today if we had taken what seemed at the time like the easier path. And following Jonathan Poneman's model, while it may have seemed "risky" to go it on our own, we also saw it as an absolutely necessary decision.

And that's the best way to view regret: to see it as the cost of *not* doing something, of not taking a risk because you're afraid. Afraid of failure, afraid of the unknown, afraid of—what? Many Leaders have challenged us with this simple question, so we'll do the same for you. When you feel yourself backing away from a risk, ask yourself: What's the worst that can happen?

EVALUATE PERCEIVED RISK VERSUS ACTUAL RISK

"There's something that climbers talk about, the difference between perceived risk and actual risk," Jim Koch, the founder of Samuel Adams, told us when we met him at his massive brewery. For Jim, the perceived risk was staggering when he left his high-status job at the Boston Consulting Group to start brewing small-batch beer. Skeptics observed him with disbelief: how could he leave a high-paying job, a great office on the thirty-third floor?

"The big risk would have been staying at a job that wasn't fulfilling, and wasting my life. That's a risk. Quitting it to do something I really loved and believed in, that's not a risk."

—**JIM KOCH**, *founder and brewmaster, Samuel Adams*

Economists are continually struggling with how to quantify risk in the financial world. One of their key tools is the opportunity cost equation, which weighs the losses and gains of different decisions.

$$\frac{\text{Cost of selected alternative} - \text{Cost of next best alternative}}{} = \text{Opportunity cost}$$

When you're in the concrete world of dollars and cents, calculating opportunity costs works just fine. But in balancing alternatives on your Roadmap, there's more nuance, since the "cost" of your decisions is based on your own individual needs and values. When you're young and free of obligations, you can couch surf and live on ramen because your opportunity costs are low. It's comparatively easy, at that stage, to live on the cheap in the service of your dream. If you have a family, or are supporting your aging parents, or have a mortgage, then your costs are higher and the balance might shift. And then there are the emotional opportunity costs—will choosing comfort over risk leave you with gut-wrenching regret when you look back in your later years?

The Adjacent Possible theory from "Drip. Drip. Splash." (page 205) is the best way to balance out a risk when it does indeed seem too costly. Maybe you can't quit your job and start that small business you want to today, but what is immediately outside of your current realm of possibility? What steps can you take to get to a point where the costs balance out in your favor?

As you come up against situations in life that call for either taking a risk or making a safe bet, remember that not taking a risk can be the riskiest thing to do. Taking a risk is a preemptive strike against regret.

So peer into the distant future for a second—envision yourself, as Cheryl did, taking your last breaths. Now ask yourself . . .

WHAT RISKS WILL I

REGRET **NOT** TAKING?

DON'T OVERTHINK IT

By Bruce Hardy

MAYBE IT WAS CHEESY, BUT SCREW IT, I WATCHED MY HAND OUTSIDE THE OPEN WINDOW OF THE RV, FEELING IT SLICE THROUGH THE COOL AIR. AS WE WHIRRED DOWN THE GREAT OCEAN ROAD ALONG THE COAST OF SOUTHERN AUSTRALIA, IT WAS DIFFICULT—NO, IMPOSSIBLE—FOR ME TO FEEL TRAPPED BY THE SAME PRESSURES THAT HELD ME DOWN SO HEAVILY BACK HOME. FOLLOWING ONE SEASIDE CLIFF FACE TO ANOTHER, THE SALT AIR BLASTED MY FACE, MY HAND CUT THROUGH THE WIND, LIKE I WAS SWIMMING THROUGH A WAVE. I WAS IMMERSED IN A SENSE OF POSSIBILITY AND PEACE. VICTORIA'S GIANT SKIES STRETCHED OUT SO FAR OVER THE PACIFIC, I IMAGINED I COULD SEE TASMANIA ON THE EDGE OF THE HORIZON. TO OUR LEFT, THE EXPAN-SIVE SEA WAS DOTTED WITH DISTANT STORM CLOUDS, BACKLIT AGAINST THE BLUE SKY. IT FELT LIKE WE WERE HANGING ONTO THE EDGE OF THE CONTINENT WITH ALL OF AUSTRALIA ABOVE US.

JUST BEFORE THE ROAD VEERED INLAND, WE PULLED OVER AND WALKED OUT ONTO THE RICKETY CLIFFTOP VIEWING PLATFORM OVER THE TWELVE APOSTLES.

I STARED DOWN AT THE MASSIVE ROCK FORMATIONS THAT JUTTED UP FROM THE SEA, THE ROLLING WAVES LAPPING AT THE SIDES OF THE ANCIENT COLUMNS. THE STORM CLOUDS SLOWLY PILED UP AT THE EDGE OF MY VISION, AND FOR WHATEVER REASON, I FELT

Born in Africa, **Bruce Hardy**, along with his family, fled war-torn Zimbabwe and immigrated to Australia. Brimming with intel-ligence and energy, Bruce struggled to balance his ambition to pursue the performing arts with his sense of obligation to his family. He knew that getting a law degree would mean security for his family, but he was truly interested in the arts. Bruce, along with two other Roadtrippers, took a Green RV across Australia looking for a fresh perspective on the courage to take risks.

MY SENSE OF PEACE RECEDE. REAL LIFE CAME POURING BACK IN LIKE THE CHANGING OF A TIDE. THAT'S HOW IT TYPICALLY WORKS FOR ME: MOMENTS OF FREEDOM, FOLLOWED BY MOMENTS OF WEIGHTED, STIFLING DISCOMFORT. ALL THE DECISIONS I NEED TO MAKE, ALL THE STRESS AND EXPECTATION, PRESS ME DOWN. AND THEN THE PARALYSIS. NOT LITERALLY, WELL, ALMOST LITERALLY . . . I FREEZE UP. I STALL OUT IN MY LIFE. CHOICE BECOMES IMPOSSIBLE.

A FEW WEEKS BEFORE THAT MOMENT, I HAD TAKEN A LEAP AND GOTTEN MYSELF ON THIS ROADTRIP. ON THE ROAD, THINGS MOVED WHETHER I LIKED IT OR NOT, BUT WHEN THE TRIP ENDED, WHAT THEN? IT WOULD BE ALL UP TO ME TO KEEP THE ENGINE RUNNING. IT WOULD ALL BE UP TO ME TO DEAL WITH THE PRESSURES I FEEL AROUND WHAT TO DO WITH MY LIFE. THE TRIP HAD ALREADY OPENED MY EYES AND SHOWED ME THAT I WASN'T TRAPPED BY THE EXTERNAL EXPECTATIONS SWIRLING AROUND ME. I KNEW I COULD MARK OUT THE DIRECTION OF MY LIFE, I JUST DIDN'T KNOW WHERE I WAS HEADED. I WORRIED THAT MY LACK OF DIRECTION WOULD BE ENOUGH TO STOP ME FROM EVER TAKING A STEP AT ALL.

AFTER OUR SCENIC PIT STOP, WE HEADED TO ADELAIDE, THE BUSTLING CAPITAL CITY OF SOUTH AUSTRALIA. WE HEADED TO THE THEATER TO MEET ACTOR/DIRECTOR JO TURNER.* IN JO, I SAW A REFLECTION OF THE VERY ISSUES I STRUGGLED WITH. FROM AN EARLY AGE, JO HAD KNOWN HE WANTED TO BE AN ACTOR, BUT THE PRESSURES OF THE NOISE DIVERTED HIM TOWARD STUDYING BUSINESS.

"I SPENT FIVE YEARS AT MELBOURNE UNIVERSITY, AND I STUDIED ARTS COMMERCE, AND THE REASON I DID THAT WAS BECAUSE MY PARENTS WANTED ME TO," SAID JO. "I HAD NO INTEREST IN IT WHAT-SOEVER. I ACTUALLY MANAGED TO GET MY DEGREE, BUT I SPENT THE ENTIRE TIME THERE JUST DOING THEATER. AND THEN I MADE A VERY CLEAR DECISION TO LEAVE AUSTRALIA AND GO OVERSEAS, CONTINUE STUDYING, AND TO MAKE THE CHOICE TO BE AN ACTOR—THAT'S WHAT I WAS GOING TO BE."

www.roadtripnation.com/leader/jo-turner

I wondered if Jo lamented the time he spent diverted from acting, but he didn't seem to see it as a mistake. Like other leaders I would meet on this roadtrip, he saw the long line of decisions that led him to where he is not as failures but steps along the way. In fact he credited Melbourne as the place he learned lessons that continue to influence his acting. "Don't be afraid to make choices," he said. "Choices bring you clarity."

"One thing I have learned is the best thing you can do is make decisions," he said. "Actually, that's the only thing you can do, is make decisions. When you vacillate and you don't make them, nothing is ever clear. Being an actor, this is what you learn all the time. You learn to trust your instincts."

Not long into the interview, Jo had us up on our feet for an improvisational exercise. Jo told us we needed to act as if my fellow roadtrippers and I were a single person. I would say one word, and then my co-trippers Kay and Brynn would say another, circling back to me, creating one fluid sentence (we hoped).

"Read me a letter" Jo told us, so we looked down at our imaginary letter, and began.

"To - Bob, Why - are - you - so - funny - and - courageous - today? - I - like - your . . ."

Silence.

I froze up.

"What were you thinking about?" Jo asked me.

Silence. I was still frozen! I couldn't respond. "There was a word on your lips, but you didn't say it. That's because your brain was trying to think of something really good, and as a result it didn't say anything. Improv is about making a choice. Don't think. Don't think for one second. Just do things, just do things, just do things."

Later, Jo shared some of his experiences from theater school with us. "There was a great moment that happened in my first year. I was in an improvisation class, and it was

RUN BY THIS MAD, FANTASTIC WOMAN FROM SLOVENIA. SHE LOOKED LIKE THE CLASSIC BAD WITCH OUT OF THE FAIRY TALE. AND SHE WAS ABSOLUTELY TERRIFYING. SO THIS SCHOOL MAKES YOU DO ALL SORTS OF STRANGE THINGS THAT YOU HEAR ABOUT LIKE 'BE A TREE,' AND ALL THIS STUFF. I HAD TO BE A LAKE. I WOULD SPEND MY WHOLE TIME IN THE FIRST MONTHS OF SCHOOL JUST WATCHING EVERYONE AND COPYING A BIT OF THAT PERSON, AND A BIT OF THAT PERSON, AND THEN I'D GET IT RIGHT. 'I'LL GET A GOOD MARK AND IT'LL BE GOOD.' AND I REMEMBER DOING THIS ONCE IN THIS CLASS, AND I'D JUST DONE MY LAKE, AND IT WAS A FANTASTIC LAKE. AND I, PROUD OF MYSELF, WENT AND SAT BACK DOWN AND SHE JUST STOPPED ME AND SAID [VERY SARCASTICALLY], 'YEAH, GOOD. YEAH, REALLY GOOD.' AND SHE SAID, 'IF YOU EVER BE FREAKING GOOD IN ONE OF MY CLASSES AGAIN YOU CAN GET OUT! IT'S BORING. YOU'RE BORING.'

"AND THEN SHE SAID, 'TAKE A BLOODY RISK! WHAT ARE YOU HERE FOR? TAKE A RISK! YOU STUDY EVERYTHING, YOU TRY TO LEARN HOW TO DO IT, AND THEN YOU DO IT WELL? THE GREATEST CRIME YOU CAN POSSIBLY DO IN THE THEATER IS TO BE GOOD. BE BRILLIANT, OR BE SHIT, BUT DON'T BE GOOD.'"

THERE WAS SOMETHING ABOUT THAT LINE. "MY ABSOLUTE WORST NIGHTMARE," I TOLD JO, "IS WAKING UP IN FORTY YEARS' TIME, LOOKING BACK ON MY LIFE AND THINKING THERE WAS NOTHING REMARKABLE THERE."

"THAT MEANS YOU HAVE TO MAKE REMARKABLE CHOICES, THEN," JO SAID. "A REMARKABLE LIFE IS MADE BY REMARKABLE CHOICES, IT'S NOT MADE BY SAFE CHOICES. THAT'S ALL. THAT'S THE ONLY THING YOU CAN SAY. IF YOU NEVER TAKE THOSE RISKS, YOU NEVER GROW. YOU ALWAYS HAVE TO TAKE THOSE RISKS, OTHER-WISE YOU WILL ALWAYS BE DOING THINGS SAFELY, WHICH IS JUST A WASTE OF TIME, THERE'S NO POINT."

JO WALKED OUT WITH US TO SIGN THE CEILING OF OUR RV,
PUTTING HIS MARK JUST OVER THE DRIVER'S SEAT. IT READ:

**"I chose this spot. I could've thought
about it for ages, but I didn't."**

—Jo Turner

WE HEADED OUT INTO THE HEART OF THE AUSTRALIAN OUT-
BACK AND I LAY ON MY BACK AND STARED UP AT JO'S QUOTE.

I DECIDED RIGHT THEN AND THERE THAT I HAD TO THINK
OF MY LIFE IN IMPROV TERMS. I HAD TO LET GO OF THE IMPULSE
TO CONTROL. I HAD TO STOP TRYING TO MANIPULATE THINGS INTO
PERFECTION. I NEEDED TO LET THINGS HAPPEN IN THE MOMENT,
AND LISTEN TO MY INTUITION. FOR JO, WITH EVERY CHOICE HE
HAS MADE, THINGS HAVE BECOME LESS HAZY. ACTION MAKES THE
BLUR OF UNCERTAINTY CLEAR.

CHAPTER 19

GET TO FAILING

Never has a letter had more maligned associations than "F." F is for failure, F is for fake, F is for fear, F is for fraud. F is for f . . . (okay, we walked into that one). It starts in school with the dreaded grade F. Getting an F means you under-performed to the fullest extent; you failed, brought shame to your name. There is no lesson to be learned, no helpful takeaway for bettering your performance the next time. It's no wonder we develop such a deep-seated fear of failure.

Oddly though, despite our fear of it, failure is just part of business as usual—the daily process of missteps and improvement that's part of getting the work done. Even though this is a bona fide fact, we still hold onto outmoded ideas about the shame and fallout of failure.

Organic life itself is the product of millions upon millions of years of trial and error—why shouldn't our lives follow suit? Without failure, you can't improve, modify, or move on. Failure is what gives you the impetus to recraft the beta version of yourself; it redirects your Roadmap. Ultimately, failure is a good thing. Before the first Roadtrip, we couldn't even fathom the idea that suc-cessful people failed. But everywhere we've been, accomplished people have shared stories of the failures that changed and improved them.

- **David Neeleman**, the founder of JetBlue, was fired from his high-level VP job at Southwest Airlines. His failures and successes at Southwest helped him create JetBlue.

- **Wanda Sykes**, acclaimed comedian, actress, and Emmy Award–winning writer, bombed on stage before she became a household name.

- **Howard Schultz**, chairman of Starbucks, approached 240 potential investors with his vision for European-inspired coffee shops—99 percent said no.

- **Jesse Jacobs**, owner of the Samovar Tea Lounge chain in San Francisco, was rejected for a business loan by seventy-one banks before finding funding.

- **Ben Zander**, conductor of the Boston Philharmonic, experienced failure at a young age when his mother entered his compositions in an arts festival. When the time came to present the awards, the judge held up Ben's work and said, "These compositions are so bad that this young man should be discouraged from ever composing again."

Video game designers often cite studies showing that during a game, the most enjoyable moment for the player is actually when they fail and are spurred to try again. You know the feeling: that moment in Tetris when the blocks stack over that top line, or Mario loses his last life, and you feverishly hit "retry" because now you know more about that level, and you know you're one step closer to beating it. Your undeterred video game brain doesn't view starting over as reason to give up, rather you see it as an exciting challenge. You keep going until you save the world (or, until your fingers cramp into a claw).

We thrive on trial and error, on solving problems and overcoming obstacles, and no reward is more satisfying than overcoming failure and seemingly insurmountable challenges. Failure incites movement, and a chance to do better.

Using failure as a tool for both self-reflection and further action is something that Paralympian and six-time world champion wheelchair racer Jeff Adams* excels at. It would be easy to slot Jeff, paralyzed at age nine during treatment for cancer, into a movie-of-the-week "I overcame my disability" story, but that's not where the true power of Jeff's story lies. And while he has never let his disability get in the way of his zeal for sports, and his unwavering determination was certainly a huge factor in his success as a Paralympian, Jeff's wisdom and growth stem from his relationship with failure.

> **"When I go out and speak to students, I talk about races I lost. Because I've learned more in losing. Those are the times when I've grown."**
>
> —**JEFF ADAMS**, *Paralympian*

One of his crucial failures was in the summer games in Barcelona. "I went into the last lap on a breakaway with two other guys, and in my head it was like, 'My life is gonna change today. The last lap is the best thing I do. I'm on a breakaway with only two other guys, and they give three medals. Mathematically, this is working!' But I made a mistake by not checking my equipment enough."

Jeff's chair broke in that last lap, spilling him face-first onto the track.

  www.roadtripnation.com/leader/jeff-adams

"I lost. It went from being the best day to the worst day. **We have it so ingrained in us that it's always about winning. Maybe it's about losing, and suffering, and overcoming, and having that courage.** But we don't value that as much as the 'win.' So, I won a race in Sydney, and it was a great day. But what did I learn? That it's fun to have a great day? That's the weird conundrum in life: You learn so much more when things aren't easy, when things aren't fed to you, when things aren't perfect."

Consider this: Failure is nothing more than a result. It may not be what you hoped for, but it is an unchangeable fact. You can't fight or hide from facts. Experiencing failure is like downloading information. It's a new fact to process. You now know something that you didn't before. Results—favorable and unfavorable—lead to new actions, more informed actions, more calculated risks, all of which move you closer to the center of your Roadmap.

So let's agree to take the "F" out of failure. In fact, let's change society's definition of the word:

The traditional definition of failure:

Let's try this instead:

FAILURE

noun ('fāl-yər)

Lack of success.
Synonymous: Nonfulfillment.
Defeat. Collapse.
Foundering. Loser.

FAILURE

noun ('fāl-yər)

A critical action in the process
of growth and the acquisition
of experience.
Synonymous: Create personal
growth. To learn. To experiment.

Think about instances in your life that you, either now or at some other time, labeled as failures. Using the new definition, list those failures here. But take it a step further. See if you can identify one—or many—lessons you learned from each failure:

FAILURE	WHAT I LEARNED

Take a look at these lists. Your failures may still make you cringe, but that's okay. Focus on what you learned and what you took away from the experience. How have you grown since then? How has your life changed in a good way? How are you doing things differently from how you were before? How are you developing and rebuilding your self-confidence to try again?

Failure itself is not bad. What's bad is the inability to learn or grow from a situation that might not have gone your way the first time. That is true failure.

Craig Brewer,* the renowned director of gritty hits like *Hustle & Flow* and *Black Snake Moan*, doubled down on this philosophy when speaking with us, urging us to seek out failure. Early in his career, he and a few friends and family members joined forces on a quest to create a masterpiece. Shirking their jobs and responsibilities in favor of pursuing their dreams, they pooled their savings together and set out to make the great American movie. How did it work out? As Craig revealed with a wistful smile, "It failed, miserably. I mean, there's close to $30,000 of film that sits undeveloped, and I don't think I'll ever develop it." That flop wasn't Craig's last. It was simply the first in a string of many failures along Craig's road.

Like Craig, we all fail. A lot.

The specter of fear that failure engenders is deep inside all of us. Craig's solution is the old stare-the-demon-in-the-eye approach. Failure is a part of life, a painful part, a rough and messy part, but an unavoidable one. So embrace it.

When Craig met with our crew, one Roadtripper, Michael, spoke with Craig about how his fear of failure was holding him back from pursuing a film career.

"Are you perfectly clear on the fact that you will fail?" Craig asked. "Are you cool with that? I mean, you know you're going to fail, repeatedly. The only way you're going to get good is if you fail. So get to failing. Get that process going. Don't put that process off, because it's going to hurt more when you're older. Because what ends up happening is people don't want that hurt, so they get married and have kids, and then they blame their families and their circumstances for the fact that they didn't want to fail. . . . **So if you want that enrichment of success, get busy failing."**

* **www.roadtripnation.com/leader/craig-brewer**

Randii Wessen, a systems engineer at NASA's Jet Propulsion Laboratory, applied for the shuttle astronaut program twelve or fifteen times in a row. He has never been accepted. In his files he has rejection letters from grad schools, internships, aerospace companies, and even the very laboratory where he now works. "You can measure the caliber of everything by how it handles adversity," says Randii. "What do you do when you get a lousy grade? What do you do when you get rejected from a university? What do you do when someone dumps you in a relationship? It's how you pick yourself up that makes you stronger, and that really tells you something about the caliber of who you are as a person." With that mantra in mind, Randii left us with a chestnut: **"Those who dare, risk defeat. Those who don't, ensure it."**

Failure is never the end of a story; it's not even really a failure. Mistakes, and even epic blunders, are helpful instruments as you make your own road. Take risks. Get to failing! If things don't turn out how you imagined, or you fall flat on your face, modify your method and try again. Failure is an outcome, nothing more. It's a series of lessons to be learned along the way to better versions of yourself.

CHAPTER 20
FIGHTING DOUBT

Our generation is caught in a vise of external validation. We're quick to measure our self-worth in Instagram likes, we hashtag our lives, craving constant approval from a long list of virtual friends. And on the other side of the equation, we've been raised in a world that tells us to value self-esteem above all else; everybody gets an award ribbon, every one of us is a unique snowflake. Why then is fighting against self-doubt so continually challenging for us? Shouldn't we be equipped to roll with the punches?

Why do we continue to feel unworthy of the things we want?

Doubt is nothing new—it's not a generational thing. From Hamlet to Holden Caulfield, fighting doubt is an old war. It begins early on, in the halls of school, on the playground, in your family home. Are your parents happy with your choices? Do you look good? Do you fit in? Are you doing things that the cool kids like? Our self-confidence gets jammed in the gears of the adolescent Assembly Line.

"My biggest poisonous habit was insecurity, second-guessing myself," says Christina Heyniger, the adventure tourism consultant we profiled in "The Blank Canvas." "I needed someone to approve of what I was doing. In high school I was such a horrible geeky dork, and I wanted so much to be popular. And when I got to college I was the same way. I just wanted to be in the right sorority, and I wanted the right people to like me. . . . I just could not be happy unless someone was going, 'You're cool!' I didn't even care what *I* thought. I just wanted to make sure all others were happy."

We've probably all learned that the herd lives and dies in high school, and we may shake off some of these insecurities when we say good-bye to our teenage selves, but the template is still set. We fall into the trap of defining our self-worth by the perceived value granted to us by outside forces. Media barrage us with images and concepts of what should make us feel good about ourselves. But none of that, not one ounce of it, has anything to do with our actual authentic selves.

The key to fighting doubt is believing in your own personal worth outside of whatever social strata or Noise-controlled constructs you happen to be cooped up in. That's hard, sometimes impossible. You cannot win the fight against self-doubt by stewing in your own thoughts. Your Roadmap helps. Taking intentional action guided by your Roadmap leads to movement, which leads to change, accomplishment, skill development, creation of meaningful communities, and a sense of satisfaction. **Self-doubt crumbles in the face of a clear understanding of yourself.**

SMALL STEPS BUILD CONFIDENCE

Like we've seen with other aspects of Self-Construction, it's okay to start small. When Megan, a Roadtripper from season ten, first sat behind the wheel of the Green RV, her anxieties were running high. The small-framed New York native took one look at the thirty-six-foot/twelve-meter behemoth and exclaimed, "How the hell am I supposed to drive that thing?" But she bucked up and turned the key. After a few laps around an empty parking lot, Megan rolled the RV out onto the busy streets of Los Angeles. A few days later she navigated the giant vehicle up California's infamous Pacific Coast Highway through Big Sur, one of the most treacherous stretches of road in the country. By the end of the trip, Megan had no problem tackling the mean (and *narrow*) streets of New York City with confidence and aplomb—assured behind the wheel of her bright green chariot.

Sometimes we have to learn what it's like to feel confident. It's the old put-a-penny-in-the-piggy-bank lesson: small accomplishments will help you get into the habit. Christina Heyniger recalled her own confidence-building process as being about sweat, literally. "The gym was the one place where I started building some confidence in something that I did," she says. "I got myself out of bed every morning at 5:00 A.M. I did this work. I had something I could be proud of. All these things are mini triumphs." Accomplishing something, large or small, helps you build the muscle memory of what accomplishment feels like.

"Once you push yourself to do something, and you see that you can do it, then you're off. Then you just keep building. But the first thing you have to change is the way you talk to yourself," says Christina.

This is an essential element of overcoming doubt: We have to become the authors of our own internal mantras and replace the toxic messages of the Noise with positive messages of empowerment. Believing in yourself takes practice, and a mantra helps.

Let's start by getting the garbage out. Examine how you talk to yourself. What are the internal statements that reflect your personal self-doubt? What Noise do you whisper to yourself? Things like: "I'm not experienced enough to have a valid opinion," or "Other people are much smarter," or "I don't belong here."

At Roadtrip Nation, the way we fight our own self-doubt is to replace that internal Noise with the voices of the Leaders we've spoken with on the road. We're often asked how we turned our initial crazy Roadtrip into what Roadtrip Nation is today. The answer is surprisingly simple: The words of the Leaders we have met have pushed us forward, eliminating quitting as an option.

Get that internal Noise out of your headspace . . . and into this space. Use the space in the illustration to write down as many self-doubts as come to mind. Now read your self-doubts aloud. Chances are you'll hear the absurdities of those statements, and once they're out of your head, you can work on any truths you may hear in them.

Here are a few words that got us through the dark moments of doubt:

"It matters so much just to follow that little whisper or voice that's in your head and your heart. That's the one. . . . You want to say, 'No, I'm going to ignore it.' But don't do it."

—**WARREN BROWN**, *baker and bakery owner, CakeLove*

"You've got your whole life before you. So what the hell are you worried about? Just believe in who you are. You know who you are. Stick with it and don't let anything get in the way of your ambition. You know? You don't have to hurt people, you don't have to be obnoxious about it, you don't have to even say it out loud. But always be dogged. Go back to it, and never let it drop. And eventually, someone will pick up on it."

—**MALCOLM McDOWELL**, *actor*

"Nobody gets through without conflict. If there was no stress or difficult situations, you'd be half a person. Whatever you're going through, you're building yourself. If you look at it that way, [you think], I am just feeling myself getting fuller and stronger, each thing that happens, so that later you can really be a genuine full person. Not just half a person, not just somebody who goes through the motions or says what people want you to say."

—**ELAINE KWON**, *concert pianist*

To suppress the doubt in your own head, pick a positive mantra and repeat it silently each time you find yourself in a moment of fruitless doubt. At first feelings of doubt will tumble out of you, but counteract them by responding with your chosen mantra. The goal is to cut off the Noise earlier and earlier.

SELF: "I'm not smart enough." RESPONSE: "I have everything in me to do this."

SELF: "I'm not smart . . ." RESPONSE: "I have everything in me to do this."

SELF: "I'm not . . ." RESPONSE: "I have everything in me to do this."

SELF: "I . . ." RESPONSE: " . . . have everything in me to do this."

If learning to deal with self-doubt is like building muscle, then that means you have to do the reps. Again and again, slowly building up the ability to believe in yourself. The lawyer Charline Gipson has taken several bold leaps in her life: moving from Jamaica to Canada with her family, going to college alone in the States when her family objected, leaving her high-powered job as a lawyer in Manhattan when it failed to satisfy, and boldly opening her own law firm in New Orleans. At none of these junctures did Charline have the big picture etched in stone, or a clear vision of where she would end up. But step by step, the repetitive power of Charline's continued risk-taking helped her move forward to the next milestone, and the next.

"In my office right now, there is a picture of me when I was in the sixth grade, the year I moved from Jamaica to Toronto," Charline says. "When I look at that picture, I start to recount a résumé of experiences where I stepped off the cliff, and the ground came up and met my foot." The more we force ourselves into intimidating situations and test what we're made of, the more confident we become that we can handle the next test. Then, after we've done it enough times, we start to take on the traits of a cat—no matter what situation we get thrown into, we know we can land on our feet because we trust ourselves.

EVERYONE FEELS IT

Even if the small cliffs are too much, if the doubt in your head is borderline crippling, remember, you're not alone. Everyone struggles with self-doubt, in varying forms, every day. Dave Banks* is an acclaimed photojournalist and filmmaker with fourteen Emmy nominations (and one win under his belt), but growing up he struggled with dyslexia that turned into a lasting and deep self-doubt about his abilities. "I was constantly called stupid," says Dave.

In an effort to find a way to understand what he was going through, and get over the doubts he had about his own creative process, he joined an artists' support group. "I had to stop thinking, 'Are they going to like it?'" Dave points out. "I needed a different perception because we can always be self-critical and we can just beat ourselves up. I needed to get beyond that. What the support group showed me was that other artists had the same feelings as I did, and the same insecurities.

"Screw confidence, just do it. The more risks that you take, the stronger your confidence grows."

  www.roadtripnation.com/leader/david-banks

Ira Glass, the host and executive producer of *This American Life* introduced in "Skills Pay Bills," shared with us some poignant insights about the power of confidence, noting that it isn't always realistic to conquer doubt, but we can manage. He explains, "Some people feel happy and confident when they wake up in the morning every day, and some people are going to feel doubt and worry. . . . And it's good to acknowledge early which kind you are and make your peace with it. I know no matter what I'm doing, I'm going to wake up worried every single day." Ira's lesson is to not let lingering self-doubt be a deal-breaker for the things you want to attempt in life.

JUST ACT LIKE YOURSELF

Doubt will never abandon us completely, but we can combat it by making considered decisions and changing our internal monologues. As it turns out, believing in yourself is a product of acting like yourself.

Julia Dalton-Brush,* a fitness guru and makeup artist who demystifies the process of losing weight for beginners and advocates for self-acceptance over mainstream society's beauty standards, underscored this "just be you" philosophy. You don't need confidence. You need action integrated with your individual values. That combo contains the seeds from which confidence grows.

"I don't even think it's about confidence; it's just doing what I love and feeling like this is exactly what I'm supposed to be doing," Julia told us. "We have a choice to be exactly who we are or put up a front. And people can feel the difference. You act differently when you're true to yourself."

*   **www.roadtripnation.com/leader/julia-dalton-brush**

279

CHAPTER 21

PRACTICE, SCHMACTICE. IT'S DOING THAT MATTERS.

Here's a confession that may be coming very late in the game: There were other road trips before Roadtrip Nation. This feels a bit like running through a list of past girlfriends with the current girlfriend, but, yes, there were other road trips—and lots of them.

Years before we set out on our first self-prescribed adventure, we were taking road trips all over the place. Up the coast to visit friends in Santa Cruz. To Utah, Idaho, and Wyoming to get to the snow. There was a road trip from Los Angeles to Seattle, then to Grand Teton National Park in Wyoming, and then back to Southern California. And we even interviewed a few people on that one.

Your soccer/swim/track coach may have told you something like "practice makes perfect," and though we all benefit from practice, our experience is that practice *doesn't* make perfect. *Doing* does. *Experience* makes perfect. To be honest, practice barely even qualifies as the start of perfect. So what were all those road trips we did before starting Roadtrip Nation? On the surface, it might sound like we were practicing, but we weren't practicing for something we had in mind for the future. We were just doing.

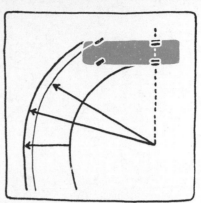

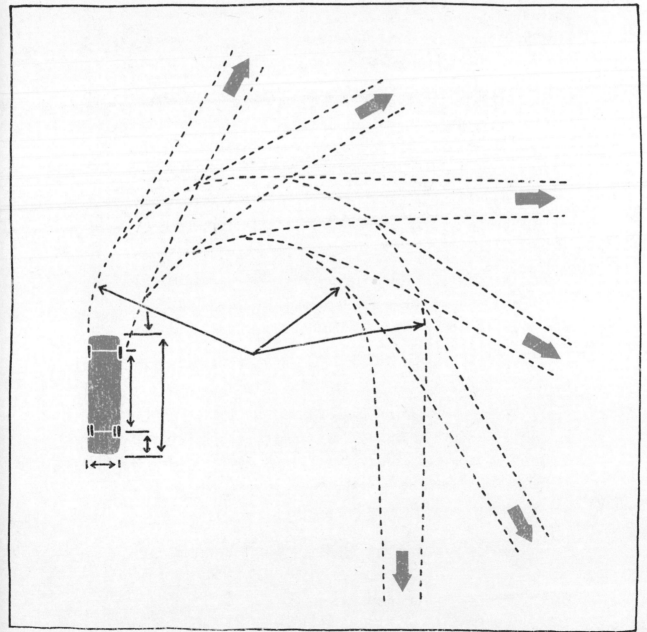

If we had actually set out to practice for Roadtrip Nation, we would have taken RV driving classes, studied up on the basics of engine mechanics, taken "how to interview" courses, studied up on what "business casual" dress code means, and forced ourselves to live in one small room for a month on a strict diet of Clif Bars and Grape-Nuts. Much like going to school, this kind of careful practice would have given us a useful logistical knowledge to build on, but it would have lacked the richness we gained from hitting the ground and experiencing. Studying theory can only take you so far. As original Roadtripper and cofounder Brian McAllister said, "Being naive and doing is better than studying and not doing."

So, how did forgoing practice pan out? Well, driving an RV with no prior experience was a bit dangerous, for a start. Dressing like who we are often made us feel out of place (we once even had to split a suit between two of us to attend a performance of the Boston Philharmonic). We never did figure out how to repair a 454 Chevy engine. And, of course, our initial interviews could have been more expertly conducted. But practicing for all that would have paled in comparison to what we learned by doing.

Veronica Belmont* sums it up best. Veronica is a technology- and gaming-centric video host whose projects range from *Tekzilla*, a weekly tech help and how-to show on Revision3, to the BBC America show *Gizmodo: The Gadget Testers*, and many more. She's an über-awesome geek who, last we checked, had over 1.7 million followers on Twitter.

Nowadays Veronica exudes a charm that belies her years of struggle. She told us, "When I was in high school and college, I had crippling social anxiety . . . I couldn't go to social events, couldn't talk to people I didn't know very well— the whole panic attack thing. I would just have total breakdowns and not be able to leave my dorm room or my apartment."

  www.roadtripnation.com/leader/veronica-belmont

In front of the camera, cracking jokes and commenting on the gaming world, Veronica's easy confidence prompts us to wonder, what gives? How'd she do it?

Veronica's change came slowly and intentionally. She found a community of like-minded people with whom she could simply be her nerdy self. Veronica admits that she still struggles with feeling uncomfortable; she just doesn't let it stop her from being out there doing. "If I'm emceeing an event or something," she says, "I'll be fine when I'm onstage, and the second I have to actually talk to the people at the event, I'm like [makes a silent awkward face]. But I think that's normal for most people, you know? So it's forcing yourself to take that extra step."

Veronica's philosophy is one we all can follow: say yes as much as possible, and act on aspirations now.

"If you're really passionate about a topic," Veronica told us, "and you want to work in that field, you should already be making YouTube videos and posting them online. You should be blogging about it. And that way, when you're ready to start applying to jobs, you already have that back catalog [of work] to show to people. Just be doing it."

She didn't say, "You should be practicing." She didn't say, "Imagine your dreams in your mind, and they will become reality." She didn't say, "Start doing" or "You should try to do." She said, "*Already* be doing." And that is the truth about the world we find ourselves in now. Today, you can get a book deal simply by posting particularly witty musings about your dog on Twitter. You can post videos of yourself singing on YouTube and land a record deal. Ten years before we started Roadtrip Nation, the only way to make a television show was to have millions of dollars of equipment, yet by the time we hit the road, equipment was cheap enough that we could cover it with one of our nearly maxed-out credit cards. This ease of access changes the level of competition. Being "successful" is not restricted to an old boys' club and a lucky few who sneaked in the door. The ivory towers have given way to a massive free-for-all, and if we're going to make it amid the fray, we need to jump in and get to doing.

"You should already be doing it."

—**VERONICA BELMONT**, *technology Web show creator and host*

ALL EDUCATION IS SELF-EDUCATION

There used to be a time when getting a college degree would set you up for life. And while it is statistically true that, on average, if you have a college degree you're more likely to be healthier and earn more and less likely to end up in jail, the guarantee that you are set for life is no more. For the first time in history, access to knowledge of all kinds is free and plentiful. This is a revolution that is difficult to overstate. The monopoly of higher education has collapsed. Today some kid living in an isolated outpost in Antarctica can jump online, tap into a million free online courses, take all the basics on Khan Academy, pick through millions of instructional videos on YouTube, gain inspiration and insights from hours of TED Talks, and become a better coder than we'll ever dream of—all by getting online and doing.

College graduates are no longer competing with other college graduates. They are competing with everyone everywhere all the time, because now anyone can access just about any knowledge they seek. Want to learn Photoshop? The day we wrote these words, there were more than 2.6 million results on YouTube for "Photoshop tutorial."

The solution? Hack your education. Add to it. Augment it. Customize all your learning around the things you're interested in. Focus on what drives you and expand outward from there. Your classes and textbooks are not enough. If you're interested in business, you should also be subscribing to *Fast Company*, *Wired*, and *Fortune*. You should be reading ten blogs, following influential people on Twitter, and meeting with people in person and online.

And if you're out of school and working, the same is true. Doing the work you're paid to do is not enough. You've got to do more to keep moving and stay abreast of the now. Read blogs, go to conferences, learn new ways to apply your knowledge and your interests. Keep building your Roadmap. No matter what you're doing, studying, or working in, it is up to you to continuously learn and expand your knowledge.

James Reeves is a New Orleans–based creative whose design collective gathers multiskilled artists, designers, and businesspeople to collaborate on projects. Reflecting on his earlier years as a freelancing designer and musician, he tells us, "You have to have a goal in mind. It's not like you're just going to sit down and say 'I'm going to learn web design.' The only reason I learned that is because we were putting out records and we wanted to tell people about them." James didn't wait to take an expensive course on web design; he approached it as a trial-and-error exercise. He learned Photoshop the same way.

When you self-initiate and curate your own set of skills, experiences, and knowledge, not just for four years of your life, but daily, you not only learn new strengths, you also stay relevant.

If you want to brew beer or start an online business or keep bees or learn Adobe Premiere or study the finer points of Dostoyevsky, you don't need to quit your job, take out loans, and go to school.

Rosemarie Certo* is a spirited first-generation Italian American and owner of the wildly popular Dock Street Brewing Co., a brewery/pizzeria in Philadelphia. She started brewing beer as a tasty libation to go with the lively dinner parties she threw for her friends. At the time, in the '80s, Rosemarie was a teacher-turned–industrial photographer, but she loved making things with her hands and started making beer and then selling it. Rosemarie didn't feel the need to be an expert; she simply began.

  www.roadtripnation.com/leader/rosemarie-certo

You can start learning and doing tonight. Hop online. Join a Meetup and talk to people who are already doing it. You don't have to be an expert to play.

"In the past it was very common for people to know how to play music, sing songs, cook, garden," says Harrell Fletcher, a Portland State University art and social practice professor. "All of these kinds of things were normal and hadn't become specialized yet to the same degree. Convenience has thrown that off, and I think specialization has thrown that off, too. In gardening or in cooking or art there's always this sense that you have to have all of these skills and all of these formalized ways of doing things or equipment or whatever it happens to be; it's something that I think ultimately alienates people from the sense that they can just do things." Knowing that we don't need permission to dive into new experiences and multiple media opens up our possibilities and proves that we can and should follow our curiosity. These pursuits not only add color and spark new interests—they can lead to full-fledged lucrative livelihoods.

What we're advocating is not a new idea. There's a word for it. It's *autodidact*.

auto (self) + didact (teach)

History is rife with examples of people who were their own professors (think Jimi Hendrix teaching himself guitar or Maya Angelou racking up literary honors without having attended college). You don't have to be a mad genius to be an autodidact; you just need to follow your own innate curiosity.

/ / / Practice, Schmactice. It's Doing That Matters. / / /

Filmmaker Dave Banks, whom we introduced a bit earlier, hacked his film school education at USC. "When I came out here to California," he recalls, "I had a suitcase and $200 in my pocket. I remember taking the bus from Burbank to USC, because USC at that time had a famous film school. Francis Ford Coppola, George Lucas, all these guys graduated from there. Well, there was no way in hell I was able to afford to go to school or get into that school because I just didn't have the grades. So I'd go to their bookstore and buy all the books that the students were selling back. That's what I studied."

Joe Quesada's* starting point to becoming the editor-in-chief of Marvel Comics was very simply loving comic books, despite having little exposure to the mechanics of the industry. "Once I knew I wanted to be in the industry," he tells us, "I started to develop a game plan. I'd missed out on this whole history of comics; it was time to get educated. Which were the better creators, which were the bad creators? I wanted to be like the better creators. That was my roadmap."

Self-study, practice, and discipline kept Joe on target. When an opportunity arose for a portfolio review at DC Comics, Joe spent six weeks hunkered down, working on his comic book portfolio. He didn't wait, he just got to doing, and while doing, he educated himself. He got the job at DC as an artist, and went on to become Marvel's chief creative officer.

  www.roadtripnation.com/leader/joe-quesada

ADD EXPERIENCE—LOTS OF IT

We now know that there's no linear path to a life of satisfaction. So it shouldn't surprise us that we won't find a path to satisfaction clearly laid out in the pages of a college course catalog. It's fair to think of your education as practice. You're learning and acquiring knowledge. You're learning how to learn, but very rarely are you doing. What goes on inside the four walls of a classroom often doesn't represent real-world realities, so it's important to build a track record of experiences to add to your baseline knowledge. Besides, if we're truly following our Roadmap and mixing our Core Interests, we need to be adept in a variety of media to support the robust lives we're after.

"The roads that most of my peers took, they were expected," recalls Delfina Eberly,* the director of data center operations at Facebook. "I come from a large Mexican family, I'm first generation, my father was a farm laborer. I wanted something different. I was searching for something to connect to." Although she had no background in the digital world, Delfina found that connection among techies and data crunchers.

Her path to a high level at Facebook was not paved by coursework alone. She took a job in a computer room at a local bank on a whim, then found she actually liked the work and started signing up for all the relevant computer courses she could find. She told us, "I never had worked with computers, and didn't have that kind of training. . . . Rather than shying away from the technology, I leaned into it. I would just sit down and figure it out. And that philosophy has really served me well, even today."

✳   **www.roadtripnation.com/leader/delfina-eberly**

One of the surest ways to stay on your path is to develop your skills and add experience—lots of it—in a variety of disciplines, keeping a deeply grounded center. This cross-disciplinary model we're talking about resembles a T, and in fact, job recruiters call this having "T-Shaped" skills. What this means is that our knowledge is both broad and deep. We have the specialized knowledge in our particular field or interest (the stem of the T), but also possess a broad set of skills that let us interact with people outside of our discipline, solving problems and building relationships (the top bar of the T). When you can connect a T to your Roadmap, steps for self-education become clear (see page 333).

DON'T GO IT ALONE

Don't think that self-education should be done in the dark of your bedroom in front of YouTube. The importance of relationships in self-education is huge. Joe Quesada took advantage of a chance encounter with a comic book artist at his day job to get his foot in the door, and Dave Banks joined a support group of artists. Harrell Fletcher continuously engages with new communities to be inspired by new ideas.

Jordin Kare is the chief scientist at LaserMotive, a company that develops technology for NASA's rockets. Despite his struggles with social anxiety, Jordin advocates the value of building strong social communities. "Hang out with good people," says Jordin. "If you spend your time with interesting people, with people who are the best at what they do, with people who are smarter or better than you, then, first of all, you keep learning things. And not just practical stuff but whole ways of doing things and ways of thinking. Second, you never get lazy. And third, you find that those same people, even after you lose track of them for twenty years, they show up somewhere else odd and they say, 'Hey, I'm doing something cool. Come over here and see this.' And lo and behold you find you're doing something that you never thought about. So, hang out with good people. It makes the rest of life a lot more interesting."

Defining your own road in life is at its heart an exercise in self-education. You are learning about yourself—your strengths, your capabilities, and not what others think they are but what you know they are. Armed with that knowledge, the journey becomes about the energy and commitment you put into it. It doesn't matter as much what school you went to or what your GPA was. What matters is what you do with who you are.

/ / / *Practice, Schmactice. It's Doing That Matters.* / / /

CHAPTER 22
WHEN TO VEER
AND WHEN TO U-TURN

The importance of building momentum in life cannot be stressed enough. One thing leads to another and doorways open the more you forge ahead, developing skills, relationships, and experience. Momentum is easy when all the dominoes start to connect. You just tap the edge of one and watch them fall into each other down the line.

But how often does that really happen?

The challenges to your own personal momentum are almost uncountable, and they are almost certainly unknowable. What is certain is that no matter who you are and how much you plan, sacrifice, and strive, you will still encounter Roadblocks, and how you react to them will define who you are just as much as the circles on your Roadmap.

The moment you hit a Roadblock is a critical decision point. Will you lie down and give up, or will you overcome the challenge and become a better version of yourself?

We know we've urged you to "get to" failure and to embrace the lessons you can learn from it, but a Roadblock is a little different from an isolated instance of failure. It could be a series of failures, or one big one. It could be a major change in your life, from flunking a class, to a health issue, to getting laid off. Or it could be the nagging sense that, no matter what choices you make, you're still misguided and lost. Whatever the Roadblock is, it's something that forces you to question your direction. In order to overcome it, face it head on. It's there in front of you, so now what?

First, relax. You're not the only one to hit a Roadblock. Adversity is useful. It's a tool that tests your convictions and validates whether you're going the right way. The double-platinum recording artist Jon Foreman, of the band Switchfoot, describes the power of the Roadblock as similar to the tension required to make a sound with an instrument: "I used to think that friction—the tension that you feel—is a bad thing. You want to cut the tension. We have medicine to try and make us feel better—everything is to ease pain in our society. Pain is the enemy. But I don't think that's true. Tension is a good thing. To be pulled tight is almost the only way to make a proper noise on a guitar or a violin." We can't have music without tension, and we can't have growth without the tension of Roadblocks.

Moments of change or growth are almost always preceded by challenging Roadblocks. It's only natural—obstacles force us to make choices. The goal is to make sure you deal with the Roadblocks with honesty and intention. Remember, we can't always trust our fight-or-flight reactions.

Be in control of your reaction. Don't panic. Don't freeze. Breathe and think. A Roadblock does not mean you'll never move forward. It means that there is a situation in front of you that requires thought and attention before you proceed.

Say you're taking a shortcut through a vacant lot, stepping over discarded tires and heaps of trash, and suddenly you run into a rattlesnake coiled up ahead. Do you look for a rock to bash it with? Or turn and run screaming the other way? Seeing only those two options, fight or flight, is the response of a caveman. Neuroscience tells us that these reactions are a result of the primitive part of our brain that still processes every threat as a life-or-death situation.

Instead of following your primitive first impulse, take time to analyze the situation. Maybe there's room to the side of the path for you to walk by without disturbing the snake, or maybe upon closer inspection it's not a rattlesnake at all but a harmless garter snake. Also consider the fact that the rattlesnake, although it could harm you, is probably more frightened of you than you are of it. Given a chance, it would much rather retreat and save its venom for a prey it can eat! There are solutions to your problem if you apply reason and turn to your Roadmap for a compass heading. This is not the moment to flee or stop trying. It's the time to take that deep breath and figure out what can be learned from meeting the challenge. Then you get to choose how to react.

All of this requires a willingness to look deeply at the root cause of the setback and to take some time to analyze what it really means for your road ahead. Look at what the Roadblock is telling you and balance it against what you know about yourself.

As a place to start, explore our online Interview Archive by theme, where you'll find interviews with Leaders who have faced the very same obstacles you may be facing (doubt, failure, financial issues, negativity, and so on).

  www.roadtripnation.com/explore/themes

After years on the road observing how people approach and conquer various Roadblocks, we've come up with a flowchart (see page 302) as a sort of shorthand for figuring out what to do about any Roadblocks you are facing. There are three basic options: you can veer, bust a U-turn, or jump the hurdle.

WHEN TO VEER

Veering means being fluid and flexible in your thinking. It means letting yourself think differently about how you might apply yourself to a chosen interest or choosing which Subjective Truths, in practice, matter the most to you. It is a side step, not a complete abandonment of your direction.

When the Roadtrippers met with *Radiolab* host Jad Abumrad, one of them, Megan, was on the fence about her future path as a teacher, after applying to more than 100 jobs without success. "I'm at that point right now where I really know that I want to teach," said Megan. "But I'm not getting any jobs. So it's kind of that uncertainty principle. And I want to figure out how to better cope with that and how to be more open to Plan B and C and D."

"Well," Jad replied, "what do you define as a teaching position? Maybe that's an elastic term and you can sort of stretch it a little bit. It may not end up looking at all like what you expect. It may shape-shift on you. And the career you thought you were heading toward becomes something very different."

That's the Roadtrip definition of veering: taking something you always considered as rigid as steel and making it bend. And that bend, that flex, can lead you to your next iteration of yourself. Once Megan stopped imagining a teaching job as one thing and one thing only, she saw a host of other possibilities. She realized she could write curricula for an educational non-profit, work with students at an after-school organization, or give historical tours at an archaeological dig site in Greece. Veering—and being bendable—expands narrow expectations and deftly dances away from the Noise of "To do this, I can only be this."

Veering is what you do when you know you have the ability to succeed in an interest area and your drive is unabated, but things aren't quite coming together, demanding that you adjust your original vision a bit. This was the case with astronomer Laura Danly.*

"As a kid, I loved seeing all the Apollo missions and Gemini missions, I wanted to go to space, I wanted to study space, there was never a question in my mind," Laura says. Laura began her career at NASA—the dream job of any astronomer. "As a child, NASA was the be-all and end-all, and here I was at the Hubble Space Telescope—what could be more wonderful than that?

"But other things came into play at that time," Laura remembers. "Most importantly, my life satisfaction; I was not happy." Laura took time to create space (you'll remember this concept from "The Blank Canvas," page 100) with several

*   **www.roadtripnation.com/leader/laura-danly**

297

weeks of trekking through Nepal. Who she was had evolved from beta version to beta version. She returned with a better understanding of what authentically made her happy—and she knew in her heart it wasn't NASA. Achieving her "dream job" wasn't what Laura's Roadmap was about (it rarely is).

Now, as a curator at L.A.'s famous Griffith Observatory, Laura plans the exhibits and planetarium shows, combining her love of science with the arts, which in the end is more in line with what became her personal Roadmap. But Laura acknowledges that nothing is static. "I've restarted half a dozen times. Six years ago I was in New York, and that was at age fifty. I was changing at fifty. I hope I'll never stop changing."

Laura's steady stream of jumps has eroded doubt and built up a stockpile of self-confidence. "I remember talking to my sister just before I decided to leave NASA, and saying, 'But I'm scared. I'm scared.' And my sister said, 'Well, what's the other side of being scared?' And I thought, 'What's she getting at? Excitement!' And the minute she said that, I knew that was true. Half of the adrenaline, half of the 'I'm scared, I'm scared!' was, 'It could be really great. I'm really excited about this! . . . So when you're scared, understand why you're scared. If it's legitimate, respect it. But if in fact a good component of your fear is, 'I don't know what's on the other side. I don't know what it could be,' then [take a] deep breath. Jump out of the plane. It'll be fine. And I've done enough leaping to know that that's true."

WHEN TO U-TURN

As the term implies, the U-turn is a complete change in course. There's no way to universally gauge the motivation for this deeply personal decision—it will be different for everyone—but there are some obvious signposts that might get you to bust a sharp U-turn. Are you loving what you do? Is it what you thought it would be? Does it feel right in your gut? Do you possess the innate skill your work requires? If you think you lack the skills, do you feel enthusiastic enough to hustle to develop that skill?

If the answers to any of these questions freak you out, remember it's never too late or too early to make the U-turn.

Nat Paynter* is the director of water programs for the humanitarian company charity: water. Previously he worked as a water and sanitation specialist at the World Bank. Before all of that, however, he left a thriving career in publishing, completely changing course to study engineering. For Nat, the signs were obvious. As he puts it, "It got to the point where I hated to fall asleep because I knew I'd have to wake up. I was on the wrong track." The sudden and early death of Nat's father played a role in his introspection as well. Nat was twenty-five at the time, and he acknowledges that he's not sure he would have woken up and changed course without the perspective that such a loss can bring.

"It was while I was going through this questioning of my career, my father [had] just died, and I was like, *I could just die*. [I realized] I don't have time to be doing something I'm not excited about. I just said, 'All right, I've gotta go be happier.'"

Nat began a complete 180 from liberal arts to engineering: This meant redoing his undergraduate degree, sitting down with fresh-out-of-high-school freshmen, and grinning and bearing it while his former coworkers got married and bought houses. But his pursuit of happiness outweighed the embarrassment of admitting a misstep.

  www.roadtripnation.com/leader/nat-paynter

An even more extreme example of the U-turn is embodied in the story of Terry Stewart,* CEO of the Rock and Roll Hall of Fame and Museum. "I have four degrees, and never had any interest in any of them," Terry says. "I did mergers and acquisitions, I was a banker, and I hated all of it, and I was miserable except in my off hours when I was chasing whatever I like to do for fun." In Terry's case, this was music, movies, comic books, and pop culture.

But one day, a devastating Roadblock changed everything: He was let go from his banking job. Although Terry wasn't happy in banking, his first reaction was despair. The ensuing tension from his unemployment snowballed. Divorce, emotional free fall, and severe economic hardship followed.

In the midst of it all, Terry found refuge by connecting with some of his true interests. He began thinking about comic books and pop culture again. Those little steps toward reconnecting with joy started to give him confidence to see beyond his situation, enabling him to apply his skills and revise his Roadmap. Eventually, at forty-four, after years of not doing what he loved, Terry became, as he put it, "Spider-Man's boss," when he became the head of Marvel Entertainment Group. Never assume that a roadblock is your downfall. It's a chance to take control. As Terry reminds us, "You don't want to be put in the position of luck making a difference in your life at a later age. Be in charge of destiny now."

  www.roadtripnation.com/leader/terry-stewart

JUMP THE HURDLE

On the other hand, maybe what's right for you is to stick to your guns. To step over the snake. To maintain your vision, stay the course, and do the work to overcome the hurdle. Maybe the resistance you're encountering is just Noise, and your skills and fervor are sufficient to hoist you over the hurdle. If your internal monologue is saying "This is what I want to do, and I will make it work," then the signal from your gut should drown out the Noise. But this doesn't mean you're guaranteed success. Pushing through the barriers requires an honest assessment of your skills and your enthusiasm for the work—and you need to recognize the sacrifice it will take to get you there.

"There were a lot of kids who had much more raw talent than I did," says Betty Cortina-Weiss, editorial director of *Latina* magazine. She told us, "Writing was always really hard for me, but I didn't care. I had to work twice as hard to do it. Yeah. I did. But I couldn't imagine working twice as hard at anything else."

Of the three options, when you jump the hurdle you're definitely choosing the most difficult option. To carry on in the face of a Roadblock, you'll likely have to defy a lot of Noise, work smarter, and embrace the shit work.

Whatever your Roadblock is (or has been in the past), use this flowchart to work out your thoughts. This chart won't include all the nuances of your unique situation, but it's a place to start.

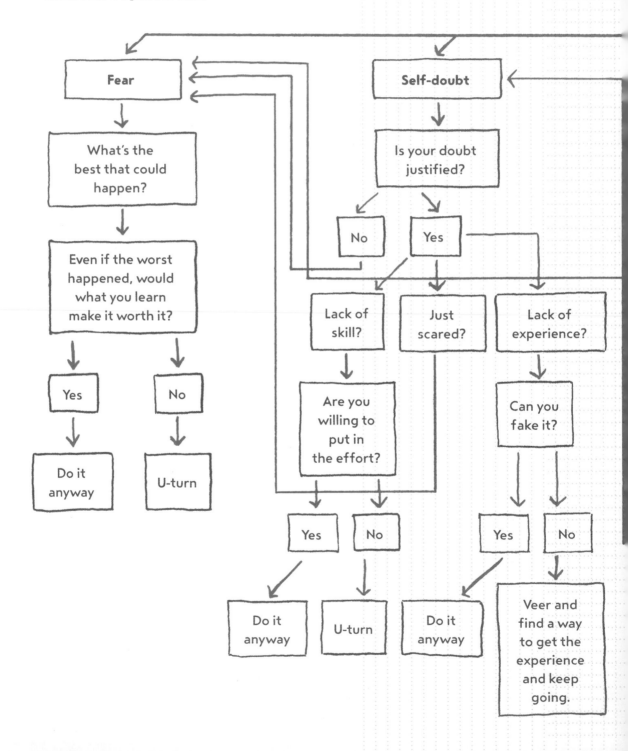

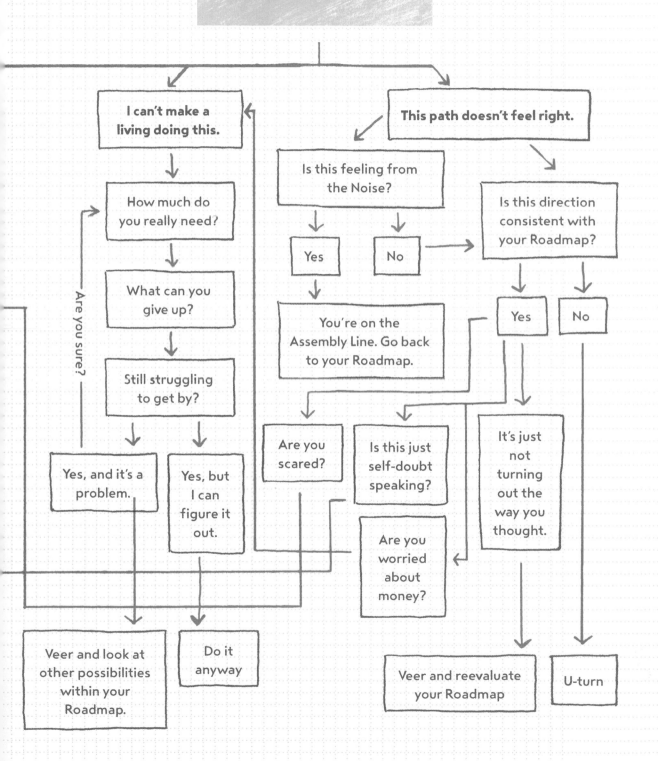

No matter how you choose to react to your Roadblocks, remember, no one but you can decode the true meaning of a Roadblock.

Liz Mandarano, the lawyer-turned–yoga studio owner from a few chapters back, reminded us that we all have keen personal intuition; it's just a matter of tuning in and listening to ourselves, regardless of what we think the herd will have to say. "One of the virtues I like best is courage," Liz told us. "I don't think it's valued that much anymore." Liz's moment of personal courage came when she found herself in her late thirties, wanting a child but with no partner on the horizon. In response to this Roadblock, she chose to stray from the conventional course and find a donor so she could become a mother.

"I was surprised at how many people came into my office and asked me how it felt to do what I was doing, and on the side said to me, 'I've always had this dream or that dream.' You think that people will think you're insane for making the decision you made and not be able to relate to you as much if you deviate from the norm or whatever the standard is, but I have found that to be completely the opposite. I'd rather fail and do what I think is right for me than not do any-thing or do what I think is safe, which isn't necessarily safe in the end."

There are Roadblocks ahead, but, as long as you're still breathing, they are not insurmountable, GAME OVER signals. They are valuable course correctors. If they never sprang up, we might thoughtlessly careen down the wrong path for years without so much as a bump or wayward piece of gravel to bounce us out of our complacency. Luckily, Roadblocks will pepper every stretch of the journey, jolting us when we need to be jolted, prodding us when we lapse into entropy, reminding us that there's more growing to do and new parts of ourselves to discover.

CHAPTER 23

DISTINCTION IS EVERYTHING

On the road one day in Vermont, after a twenty-four-hour drive and our seventh and final interview of the day, we met with Michael Jager,* the cofounder and creative director of JDK Design, the design firm behind Burton Snowboards and other clients like Xbox, Merrell, and Virgin Mobile. He evoked a quiet confidence that seemed, unlike with so many others, to come not from a manufactured act, but from his core—he was simply being himself.

Michael summed up all that we were hoping to find on the road. He began with an observation that has become, after the thousand-plus interviews we've done, a universal trait we've recognized in people living meaningful lives. In Michael's words, "If you look at examples of people who have been successful—not monetarily successful, but wholly successful in their lives, they are generally distinctive individuals. And it can be a farmer in the boonies of Vermont or Montana, or it can be the most progressive artist in New York City. They will both have self-confidence in what they're doing, and they'll have a point of view. They'll have a philosophy that they'll back up."

As Michael said, **"Distinction is everything."**

  www.roadtripnation.com/leader/michael-jager

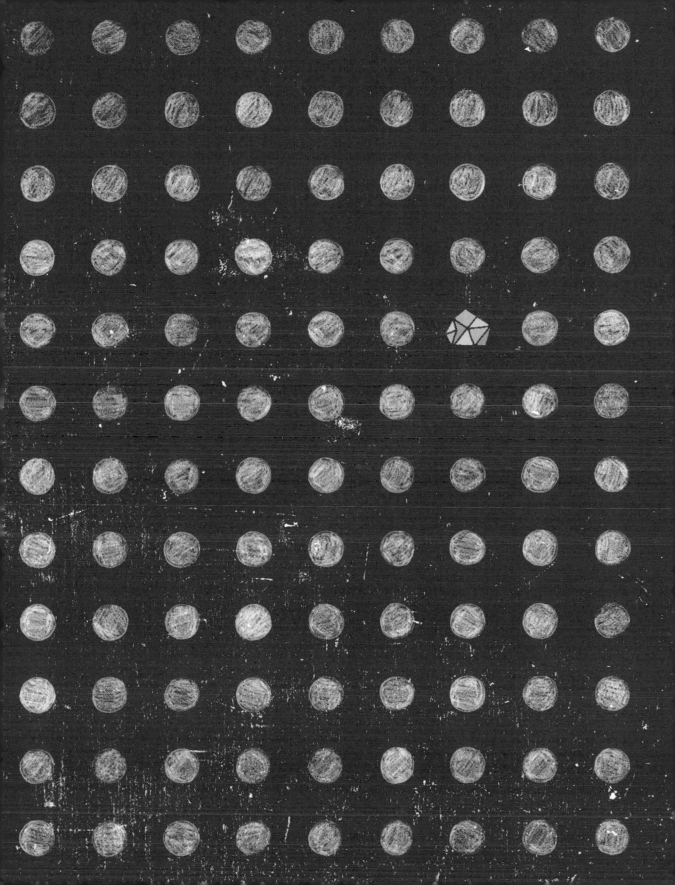

"If you decide you're gonna be a sculptor, or you decide you're gonna be an architect, or you decide you're gonna be a kick-ass accountant, if you really believe it, and you wear it on your shoulder, and you really do it with distinction, the world will conspire to support you."

—**MICHAEL JAGER**, *cofounder and creative director, JDK Design*

Knowing who you are and unabashedly chasing the things that reflect your true sense of self—these are the fundamental elements that break us free from the Assembly Line and support us as we forge our own roads in life. It's only when we take a stand on behalf of our identity that we're able to rid ourselves of the dissonance and discontent that plagues so many of us. How can life be meaningful and satisfying if it doesn't reflect who we really are?

Looking back at our meeting with Michael, we now know that the quiet self-confidence that we witnessed in him stemmed from his unwavering conviction. He knows who he is, and at every crossroad, he allows his sense of self to point him in the direction that is best for him.

Zen Master Bon Soeng told us, "The greatest gift you give to the world is when you discover who you are and you manifest that." There's joyous freedom in that statement. You don't have to find a cure for cancer. You don't have to make the *Forbes* list of wealthiest people. You don't have to be the next Elon Musk or the next Sheryl Sandberg. Being the most authentic person you can be is a gift to you, your family, and the world at large, because the life you lead will be authentically yours.

Out on the road, listening to people like Michael—these distinctive individuals who act with intention and spirit—people with a point of view, it's impossible not to begin to imagine the best versions of ourselves. Once we accept that real fulfillment is possible, the only thing that makes sense is to throw ourselves entirely into the pursuit of it. Staring out the window between interviews we daydream of all the things we'd be doing in an ideal world. We dream of our most authentic and inspired selves. It's our hope that at some point between these pages, your own daydreams tumbled out of hiding and began to look like real possibilities. That's one of the most valuable lessons from the road: **A person can only be as great as the dreams they allow themselves to have.**

"No matter what you do, you've got to use as much energy and brain power as you've got, to do it as well as you can do it, all the time. Because you don't get the days back. You don't get the hours back. You don't get the minutes back. Do the things that make you feel like you've spent your time well, and at the end you'll be happy, if not proud of your life. That's what I think about more as I get older: what are you going to think when you finally have to answer, 'Was your life spent well enough?'"

—**ANDREW LINS**, *conservator, Philadelphia Museum of Art*

The most well-spent and fulfilled lives begin with dreams, because without them, we're not truly ourselves—we're what others tell us we can be. Your vision for yourself is a start, but of course it's nothing without action. Whenever a new generation of Roadtrippers returns from the road and passes on the keys to the Green RV, they too must put their dreams into action. Realizing what's possible is both an affirmation and a provocation to grab the reins, to dive in, to try something that pushes your sense of self to the next version.

Just like each of our Roadtrips comes to a bittersweet end, this book has run out of pages. So, what have you begun to imagine yourself doing? Have you let yourself believe that what you dream isn't just possible, but inevitable? Because now it's time to own it—it's time to put your dream on the street.

"Attempt the impossible. DO THE CRAZY. Stand on a limb, and teeter. I say teeter away! Reach! Leap! ATTEMPT THINGS THAT EVERYONE SAYS CAN'T BE DONE. Run! Jump! Move. Walk. Get your crazy done! You are your bravest self. And when I say brave, I don't mean the quiet courage that it takes to raise a child, I mean the COURAGE TO DO WHAT NO ONE ELSE IS DOING. These are the years to climb a mountain! These are the years to break an arm. These are the years to fall in love, and recover, and fall in love again, and recover. Make love in a hundred different cities, shave your head, or TAKE A YEAR OFF FROM YOUR LIFE TO DO SOMETHING THAT MAKES NO SENSE TO ANYONE ELSE! Do it. Do it. Do it now! Live it! If you want to write, if you want to make film, anything you want to do—you have to live to be able to do it first. SO LIVE! LIVE! LIVE! LIVE! LIVE! Get it out of your system so that when you have an ankle that is sore, and you have bills to pay, and you have a kid to watch at night, that there are no regrets behind you. THE HEAVIEST THING YOU'LL HAVE TO CARRY AS YOU MOVE FORWARD IS REGRET. Make sure you're not carrying too much."

—STACEYANN CHIN, *poet and memoirist*

PROJECTS

As we've done our best to lay out in this book, finding the Open Road happens in the act of doing; that's where momentum builds. Self-Construction is a continual process rooted in action, and while you likely took small steps as you read each chapter, we also wanted to provide some bigger, bolder opportunities for action.

The projects that follow aren't recipes in a cookbook; they're more like open-ended lab experiments meant to help you take action with your Roadmap. They will help you discover whether an interest truly connects with who you are; they'll reinforce positive aspects of the path you're on and will help you sidestep the distractions and roadblocks. We've left room for you to keep notes as you start thinking about each project.

The level of effort you put into these is for you to decide. You can dip a toe in, you can dive in headfirst, or you can use these to help solidify your own ideas about your Roadmap. Do one, do them all, or use them as inspiration to make up your own.

Just be doing.

PROJECT #1: BLOG YOUR INTERESTS

TIME COMMITMENT: Low to medium

COSTS: $0

SET-UP TIME: One hour

TOOLS/SUPPLIES: Easy access to the Internet

GOAL: To immerse yourself in your Core Interests and share them with others

BIG IDEA: Don't wait for permission or a paycheck to start getting involved with what you love. A blog is an easy, no-risk way to become more closely attuned to your interests and articulate your singular perspective. It doesn't have to be a word bank (though it can be); it could just be a repository of photos and links to things that inspire you.

Levels of Engagement

LOW: Post photos or share links.

MEDIUM: One thoughtful post a month.

HIGH: Frequent posts with in-depth analysis.

RELATED CHAPTERS: *8, 10, 13, 14, 15, 19, 21, 23*

Here are some questions to think about before you start your blog:

1. WHO IS THIS BLOG FOR?

First and foremost, this blog is for you. It's to get you in the habit of thinking and living within your Core Interests and your Foundation. It is also about practicing and creating a body of work that you can leverage for the future. This is a place to test things out, learn what works, and gain exposure in the field that interests you—don't worry about making it perfect.

2. WHAT DO YOU PLAN TO BLOG ABOUT?

Look at your Roadmap. What subjects manifest from the intersection of your Core Interests? What unique take do you have on those combined subjects?

3. WHAT KIND OF BLOG DO YOU WANT TO CREATE?

If you're great at writing, then opt for some longer-format stuff. If you dislike writing, go for more of a light copy, image/link combination.

4. WHAT UNIQUE PERSPECTIVE WILL YOU BRING TO YOUR BLOG?

There are a million blogs out there, and while your goal here isn't to create the next *Huffington Post*, you do want to stand out—even if it's just to the three people who read your posts and that future employer who looks it up to learn more about who you are and what you have to offer.

Choose a Blog Service

Do some research to determine which blog service is best for you. Here are a few widely adopted and reasonably easy-to-use examples. *[Disclaimer: Of course, anything we've written here about technology might have evolved by the time you read this.]*

▶ **Blogger:** Great for beginners who just want to get started.

▶ **WordPress:** For those who like, above all, to write.

▶ **Tumblr:** Better for shorter-format writing, and more adaptable for a variety of different content.

▶ **Medium:** Simple and clean. Subject matter here tends to be more tech-sector focused.

Commit to a Frequency

Pick an interval of time that you can commit to. Post once a day, week, or month. Whatever it is, set a goal and stick to it.

START SOMEWHERE

Even if you feel like you have no idea what you're talking about, just post something to get started—it could simply be an open confession of your ignorance. Every successful blog has that shaky first post. Here are a few humbling first posts from now-great blogs:

Design*Sponge
When founder Grace Bonney started Design*Sponge a year out of college, she didn't envision she'd one day pay her bills with it. First intended to be a simple online portfolio, the blog soon evolved into a space for Grace to share her design inspirations, and it gained such a rabid base of followers that she was able to turn it into a full-time job. Now Grace has written a book, runs national workshops, and freelances for some of the most respected publications in the design world. But check out her first post, from before Design*Sponge was dubbed the "*Martha Stewart Living for Millennials*":

www.designsponge.com/2004/ 08/a-few-of-my-favorite-things.html

Dooce.com
Dooce is the creation of writer and web designer Heather B. Armstrong, who started a blog so she could write about things like music, pop culture, and her dog's attempts to eat things off the kitchen counter. What started as a side passion project eventually turned into a livelihood, and the income generated from Dooce has even allowed Heather's husband to quit his office job to run the business side of things. Take a look at Heather's first post, before she realized she could make a living sitting in pajamas all day long:

www.dooce.com/2001/05/06/thinking/

Decor8
This interior design blog has become a go-to source of inspiration for those seeking creative lifestyle ideas, but author and interior stylist Holly Becker was just working on her certificate in interior design when she started it:

www.Decor8blog.com/2006/01/09/ decor8-welcome/

A Beautiful Mess
ABM has snowballed from a small, meticulously curated lifestyle blog of recipes, DIY projects, and inspiration into a must-have app for any proper skinny jean–wearer. Here's a peek at their humble beginnings:

www.abeautifulmess.com/ 2007/07/w-is-for-welcom.html

Some Tips

▶ **Better to under-promise and over-deliver.** This should be fun, but if you take on too much, you'll likely get overwhelmed. Best to start out small and infrequent and then grow into it as your interest ramps up.

▶ **People love pictures.** Try to include an image for each post. Don't consider yourself an Ansel Adams? You don't have to use your own pics; just use photos from Flickr users who allow the free use of their images through Creative Commons. Go here: www.flickr.com/search/advanced/ and select the option to search for photos with the Creative Commons license.

▶ **Be unique. Yourself. And no one else.** Sure, you can model what you create by looking at the blogs that you like but be sure to bring something uniquely you to the table.

▶ **Inspiration.** Here are some blogs we love that should provide some fodder for your own blog:

Oh Happy Day: www.ohhappyday.com

Swiss Miss: www.swiss-miss.com

Boing Boing: www.boingboing.net

All Things Go: www.allthingsgomusic.com

The Sartorialist: www.thesartorialist.com

A Little Batty: www.littlebatty.tumblr.com

Conscientious Photography Magazine: www.cphmag.com

The Great Discontent: www.thegreatdiscontent.com

Brain Pickings: www.brainpickings.org

Mental Floss: www.mentalflossr.tumblr.com

Catsparella: www.catsparella.com

EdSurge: www.edsurge.com

Booooooom: www.boooooom.com

PostSecret: www.postsecret.com

Reflection

Once you have a few posts under your belt, take a moment and think back about what you're learning from this experience. Heck, these reflections could even become blog posts of their own.

1. *How does it feel to put your thoughts and ideas out there? What excites you? What scares you?*

2. *Did your curiosity around your Core Interests grow (keep going) or weaken (swap it out for another)?*

3.. *How can you use your blog as a way to engage with other like-minded individuals?*

4. *In what ways can this blog be a launching pad for the things you want to do in the future (job interview fodder, meeting new people, etc.)?*

PROJECT #2: SELL YOUR GOODS/ SERVICES ONLINE

TIME COMMITMENT: Medium to high

COSTS: $0 to $$$

SET-UP TIME: +/– five hours to get rolling

TOOLS/SUPPLIES: Variable; a camera and computer, a collection of goods or services you want to put out into the world.

GOAL: Capitalism! Nah, just kidding. Well, sort of. But truly, there's nothing like getting paid—even on a small scale—for doing something you love. If people are willing to pay for what you're selling, and what you're selling is at the center of your Roadmap, then it is validation that you're going in the right direction.

BIG IDEA: This is a perfect project for makers and doers; whether it's train whistles, custom furniture, your editing and writing services, screen-printed T-shirts of your golden retriever, or snapping wedding photos. Or perhaps you're less of a maker and really into buying and selling vintage sunglasses— the idea is to get out there and let people respond to your vision. And it doesn't have to be things. You can put your services up for sale on a freelance site or contribute to collaborative projects on sites like Quirky.com. This is how you put your dream on the street (or on the Internet).

Levels of Engagement

LOW: Make one thing, or describe your talent, and open your store.

MEDIUM: Make a few things and see what happens.

HIGH: Build a whole brand identity around your products or services and then market 'em, and unleash 'em for all to enjoy.

RELATED CHAPTERS: *3, 8, 9, 11, 13, 14, 15, 21, 23*

Before you put your goods and services in the world, here are a few questions to think about:

1. WHAT CAN I MAKE/DO?

What things are made or done at the center of your Roadmap? Chances are, if you're doing this project, you've already got something in mind. And if you don't, no worries. Start thinking about how your Roadmap can fill a specific public need.

2. HOW MANY THINGS SHOULD I MAKE BEFORE I OPEN MY STORE?

Best to start with at least one. But the truth is, you can start with zero. If you lack the upfront cash to get you started, look at Kickstarter! It's filled with thousands of projects that are sold before a single thing is made.

3. WHAT INTERESTS ARE YOU MAGNIFYING?

The goal isn't as much to make money (just yet) as it is to experiment with what it feels like to put your work out there. The idea of being a painter is one thing, but what is it like to be a painter? This is your low-touch way to answer that question.

4. WHAT IS UNIQUE ABOUT THE THING(S) YOU'RE MAKING/DOING?

The market is glutted with the same products and services, so what's unique about your work? The way you package it, how it looks and feels? Or the story behind it?

Choose a Venue

There are tons of different storefronts out there you can use. The obvious one is Etsy, but there are others geared toward specific interest verticals.

▶ **Etsy:** Offers users their own digital storefronts to sell goods; mostly geared toward those who make handmade things.

▶ **Storenvy:** Similar to Etsy: open a storefront; sell anything from organic spa-style face masks to iPad cases.

▶ **Quirky:** Collaborate on product development. Easy way to jump in without having to do everything.

▶ **Kickstarter:** Crowdsource funding for creative projects that run the gamut of ideas.

▶ **Society6:** Have apparel and products made from your designs without having to invest your own money.

▶ **Squarespace:** This easy-to-use web-hosting platform provides slick design templates for portfolios, storefronts, and blogs.

▶ **Brick-and-mortar:** Tap your local craft fair, farmers' market, or other small outlet.

Put It Out There

Once you're ready, it's time to make people aware of what you have to offer. Start with the easy: friends. Go word of mouth and share it through your social media networks. Write to bloggers who have similar interests and see if they'll spread the word.

Some Tips

▶ **Start Small.** Keep it easy. Start with a few products. See what interests people. Watch how they react to what you have and iterate from there.

▶ **Tell a Story.** As you work on your store, think of the entire experience as a story: your story, and the story of how these things have come to be made. People like to know the history of their goods, and they want to feel like the things they're buying aren't just things, but a bigger vision that says something to the world. Think about how you can highlight an aspect of your product that makes you stand out from someone doing the same things. Maybe your old-timey-styled letterpress greeting cards are created on a vintage letterpress owned by your great-grandfather; maybe the materials for everything you make are locally sourced; or maybe you donate 10 percent of your proceeds to a worthy cause. Those unique elements will invest the consumer and differentiate you from the herd.

▶ **Be Aware.** It takes a special type of person to like the entire process of creating, from building something, to marketing it, selling it, and dealing with feedback. As you go through this experience, observe the things you like and dislike. If you dislike enough of the process, start to look at how you can focus your life around the parts you do like.

▶ **Going Bigger?** If you're getting some good results, take it more seriously. There are hundreds of books on how to run a successful Etsy store, and Etsy encourages you to join Etsy teams (**www.etsy.com/help/article/332**) to get feedback and learn more from other sellers.

Inspiration

To show you how it's done and to get you motivated, take a look at a few stores we patronize. Remember that you don't have to go it alone; sites like Threadless or Cotton Bureau rely on the creative output of a wide community of people—and it's easy to use their services (and those like them) to test the waters.

Joey Roth: www.joeyroth.com

Tuts and Crash: www.etsy.com/shop/TutsandcrasH

Gemma Correll: www.society6.com/artist/gemmacorrell

Threadless: www.threadless.com

Jon Contino: www.Society6.com/artist/joncontino

Cotton Bureau: www.CottonBureau.com

Bandcamp: www.bandcamp.com

Retrofit Comics: www.retrofitcomics.com

Yellow Owl Workshop: www.yellowowlworkshop.com

Reflection

Now that you've given it a shot, what are your thoughts about getting your work out there?

1. *What have you learned about your work process through building the store?*

2. *What part of the process did you like the most (conceptualizing, designing, making, teaching, the logistics)?*

3. *Did your hunger for your Core Interests grow or weaken?*

4. *Which part of the store would you like to improve? Which part is working well?*

PROJECT #3: TRAVEL TO A NEW PLACE

TIME COMMITMENT: Partial day or longer

COSTS: $0 to $$$

SET-UP TIME: A few evenings of planning plus the length of the stay

TOOLS/SUPPLIES: Map, computer, camera, maybe a notebook and a pair of snazzy sunglasses

GOAL: To get in proximity to what you want, sometimes you need to create distance between you and your routine. The idea is to put yourself in a new headspace by visiting a new locale that lives and breathes your Roadmap or at least corresponds to a Core Interest or two. It doesn't have to be a glamorous destination; it's just about seeing things in a new light.

BIG IDEA: Take something you're interested in and seek out a location or an event that supports that interest within your time and budget. Get out of your comfort zone. Maybe it's a visit to the Maker Faire in the Bay Area to see the latest in gadget wizardry, or it could be a day-long field trip to see *The Starry Night* by van Gogh in New York City. What matters is finding a way to go somewhere new where the things you're interested in are thriving.

Levels of Engagement

LOW: Take an afternoon adventure.

MEDIUM: Make the most of a weekend trip.

HIGH: Turn your next vacation into a full-fledged Core Interest exploration.

RELATED CHAPTERS: *2, 7, 8, 9, 14, 16, 19, 22*

Before you start, here are some questions to consider:

1. THE CORE INTEREST FROM MY ROADMAP THAT I'M EXPLORING IS:

_____.

2. I'M WILLING TO INVEST $ _____ IN THIS EXPERIENCE.

3. HERE ARE FIVE PLACES THAT SUPPORT MY INTEREST THAT I'M ABLE TO TRAVEL TO WITHIN MY BUDGET:

1.

2.

3.

4.

5.

4. HOW WILL I GET THERE?

a. *Feet*

b. *Bicycle*

c. *Public transportation*

d. *Car*

e. *Boat*

f. *Plane*

g. *All of the above*

PLANNING RESOURCES

Meetup Find people gathering in almost any city in the world, based on common interests.

Lonely Planet Travel resources for places to stay and visit.

Couchsurfing Find a cheap place to sleep and interact with locals.

Airbnb A step up from sleeping on a couch, while still meeting locals.

Once you've narrowed down your list from five spots and settled on one, here's a mini photo scavenger hunt to make this trip more focused. Want to share your experiences with your fellow readers? Share your photo scavenger hunt online and use the hashtag **#RoadmapBook**:

▶ Trip planning: Take a screenshot of your Google Maps route, snap a pic of you drawing on a physical map, document your hotel reservation, your three Lonely Planet guidebooks, and anything else that completes the picture (pun intended).

▶ Share a photo that represents your Core Interests in this new place.

▶ Share pictures of people who are getting paid to work at something directly connected to the Core Interests and/or Foundation on your Roadmap.

▶ Get out of your comfort zone and try a food you've never had before. Could be a specific dish you've never tried or a staple that reminds you of your mom's home cooking. Capture the rusty street cart serving bacon-wrapped hot dogs or a foreign candy bar you've never heard of.

▶ Take a photo of a moment where you felt you were out of your comfort zone.

▶ Make a self-portrait in which the expression on your face sums up the experience you had in this new place.

Inspiration

Here are a few examples of locations that live and breathe a particular interest. Ideally you'd head out to the epicenter of your interest, but if you can't take the time or spend the cash, find your local equivalent.

▶ **Austin, TX:** Live-music capital of the world.

▶ **Los Angeles, CA:** Dive into space at the Jet Propulsion Laboratory in Pasadena and Griffith Observatory in LA. Then head over to SpaceX head-quarters a bit farther to the south.

▶ **Rome, Italy:** This city is an ultimate mix of architecture and history. From the Colosseum, built in 72 A.D., to the Pantheon, the Vatican, and Baths of Caracalla, Rome is awash in the past.

▶ **Washington, DC:** Museums. History. Politics.

▶ **Orange County, CA:** Center of the action-sports industry with companies like Quiksilver and Volcom tucked into the warehouses just off the coast. P.S. We're here, too!

▶ **Silicon Valley, CA:** Technology and start-up capital of the world.

▶ **Marfa, TX:** An unlikely modern art mecca in the West Texas desert.

▶ **Paris, France:** Plunge into the art scene at the Louvre, one of the world's largest museums that also was once a palace. Then saunter down idyllic cobblestone streets to such landmarks as the Musée d'Orsay, the Centre Pompidou, and Rodin Museum.

▶ **St Louis, MO:** Visit the City Museum if you're into creating immersive interactive experiences.

▶ **Hong Kong, China:** The Hong Kong Science & Technology Parks are home to all things engineering, science, and just about anything techy.

▶ **Nagoya, Japan:** The center of the auto industry in Japan. Like Detroit in its heyday.

▶ **Milan, Italy:** Widely considered the global capital for fashion.

▶ **Queenstown, New Zealand:** The center point for extreme sports.

▶ **Florence, Italy:** The mecca of art history and the birthplace of the Renaissance.

▶ **Zurich, Switzerland:** One of the world's main hubs of international banking and finance.

▶ **Nairobi, Kenya:** This prominent social center is full of international aid and development organizations, including United Nations Environment Programme and the African headquarters for the UN.

Grab a few magazines or sift through a few blogs related to your Core Interests. Where are the hot spots for your interests? What are the names and places that keep popping up? Maybe it's New Orleans for jazz or Portland, Oregon, for coffee. If there's a way to get close, take a tour of a facility or just be immersed in the environment of people engaged in worlds that align with your Roadmap.

Reflection

After your outing, take some time to look back on the experience. Here are a few questions to think through:

1. *How did it feel to get out of your comfort zone and dive into someplace new?*

2. *Reflect on what it was like to see people living lives built around your Core Interests.*

3. *What did you like and what didn't you like about the Core Interest(s) you explored?*

PROJECT #4: CREATE YOUR OWN SEMESTER

TIME COMMITMENT: As long as it takes, but we'll call it a semester

COSTS: $0 to $$$

SET-UP TIME: A few hours' planning, and then the number of hours you want or need to invest in classes, practical applications, and sharing

TOOLS/SUPPLIES: Depends on the type of class you create and your own budget

GOAL: To create your own immersive experience to learn and develop skills that tie into or support your Roadmap

BIG IDEA: Create your own "semester" in which you learn what you want to learn, experience what you want to experience, and are challenged in a way that you want to be challenged. Design an experience that is right for you and that connects to your Roadmap. Do it on your own time and within your own budget.

Look at your Roadmap. Create your semester based on a mashup of your Core Interests and Foundation. Focus on the overlaps of all three. How can you fill in the gaps of your expertise and accumulate skills on your own time in your own way?

Levels of Engagement

LOW: Complete an online course on a subject, skill, or topic aligned to your Core Interests.

MEDIUM: Complete an online class aligned with your Core Interests with a final project/demonstration of your learning.

HIGH: Take multiple classes aligned with your Core Interests, combined with any of the other projects or experiences, with a final project or demonstration of your learning.

RELATED CHAPTERS: *5, 8, 9, 13, 21*

The Core Interest category I want to pursue:

Before you start, here are some questions to consider:

1. WHAT DO I WANT TO LEARN?

It can be as small as learning a new program or as large as learning a new language. Work the answer to this question into a statement such as "I want to learn how to letterpress postcards" or "I want to learn how a social media strategy is developed."

2. HOW MUCH TIME DO I HAVE TO DEDICATE MYSELF TO THIS? ARE WE TALKING NIGHTS AND WEEKENDS FOR A FEW MONTHS OR JUST A WEEKEND PROJECT?

3. HOW MUCH MONEY DO I WANT TO INVEST IN THIS?

Semester Design

▶ **The Coursework**: Figuring out the content area of your semester is the first place to start.

▶ **Online Classes:** There are hundreds of online sites dedicated to providing free and open coursework. From renowned universities to no-budget YouTube tutorials, there's an endless range of possibilities to help you learn information or develop new skills. Most free, open online courses require completion of assignments, or assigned reading (usually online articles), and possibly online discussions with others enrolled in your class. Browse around and find classes that are most relevant to your Roadmap.

▶ **My Classes**

_____

_____

_____

_____

_____

Here are a few places to get started selecting free, open online coursework:

Coursera
Offers courses from more than 80 different schools

edX
Courses with a focus on art, technology, and science

Udacity
Courses with a focus on new technology, modern programming, science, and critical thinking

Khan Academy
Courses with a focus on chemistry and other sciences

Peer 2 Peer University
Online courses meant to work hand-in-hand with traditional education

Udemy
An online platform that allows professors to host open courses

Skillshare
A community-based marketplace for professionals and teachers to share their skill sets

General Assembly
A platform that connects professionals with learners in creative fields

Academic Earth
Offers 750 courses from a variety of schools

OpenCourseWare Consortium
Offers a broad range of courses

Lifehacker Night School
Online platform for aspiring coders

Required Reading

Every class you take in a traditional school setting has required reading, so why not add some to your nontraditional semester? Whether it's buying yourself a subscription to a magazine; creating a space online to track articles, op/eds, or stories you'd like to read; or even following a relevant blog, you can supplement your online coursework with as much outside content as you have time for—or can afford.

Instead of spending a ridiculous amount of money at a college store on textbooks, just think what $100 at a local bookstore will buy—or make a list of materials to check out from the local library or tap into Google Books.

▶ **My Reading Materials**

_____

_____

_____

▶ **Mentorship/Apprenticeship**

Rather than just being a receptacle for information, put your learning into action. Find a mentor in a related field, or see if you can volunteer your time at a business or organization that interests you. Look for an internship or, if you like film, find a student project that you can volunteer for.

▶ **Possible Mentors**

_____

_____

_____

_____

_____

▶ What's My Final?

You want to have something to show for all the learning you are committing yourself to. Maybe it's a new art piece for your portfolio, a new skill on your LinkedIn profile, a physical display of what you have been crafting, building, or drawing, or a presentation you'd like to give to someone in the field. Regardless of what you decide, make a commitment to complete it.

My final is _____ Due _____

Electives

Since this semester can be pretty much whatever you want it to be, we want you to think big. Here is a suggested menu of experiential activities you can choose from if you want to add depth to your coursework. You can also look for ways to use other projects in this book to work within your semester:

▶ Join a group, organization, or Meetup of like-minded people interested in learning the same thing.

▶ Follow someone on any social media outlet.

▶ Travel to a new place, your own "study abroad" equivalent.

▶ Talk to someone in your Core Interests field.

▶ Take an online class or do a tutorial in something outside your "field of study."

▶ Start a YouTube channel.

▶ Create an online forum.

▶ Create a yearbook of photographs recording your progress.

▶ Try to teach what you learned to someone else.

▶ Take a field trip!

▶ Watch some TED Talks or films that connect to your vision.

▶ Get crafty! Use your hands to create a visual representation of what you're learning.

▶ Design an infographic.

▶ Volunteer at an organization related to your Core Interests.

Reflection

Consider this your course evaluation. Take some time to think about how your semester helped you align with your Roadmap or revealed course corrections you need to make.

PROJECT #5: FIND YOUR NICHE

TIME COMMITMENT: One to ten hours a month

COSTS: $0 to $$

SET-UP TIME: Two hours

TOOLS/SUPPLIES: A computer, some form of transportation (to meet people, unless you're going virtual), and a readiness to talk to and learn from others

GOAL: To find, create, or join a community of like-minded people involved in at least one of your Core Interests whom you can learn from and exchange ideas with

BIG IDEA: Look at your Roadmap and try to find (or create) the community at the intersection of your Foundation and Core Interests. We all have a skill, either one we're just starting to explore, or one we're fairly confident we can grow into. A big part of learning is surrounding yourself with dedicated people of similar interests who can join you in a collective effort to grow. By sharing and swapping tips in a setting like this, you will not only expand your capabilities but also get the lay of the land (industry, company, and so on). Reach out to fellow enthusiasts and become better together, whether you're exploring your interest in yoga, knitting, blogging, web design, guitar, or World of Warcraft.

Levels of Engagement

LOW: Find an online forum you can contribute to that is centered around your interest or skill. We could list some here, but there is actually a message board for every interest (we just found one for jellyfish farming!).

MEDIUM: Create a members-only Facebook group, compile a mailing list, send out a monthly newsletter. Join an existing gathering.

HIGH: Start a group of your own on Meetup.com or elsewhere, create flyers and put them on car windshields, or just find a group that you can commit to with real-life people.

RELATED CHAPTERS: *8, 10, 11, 13, 14, 15, 16, 20, 21*

Before you start, here are some questions to consider:

1. ARE YOU MISSING SOMETHING? WHAT INTERESTS DO YOU HAVE WITHOUT ANYONE TO SHARE THEM WITH?

You probably have a few interests that you've never explored fully because they're not the type of things your friends are into. Try to think deeply about the untapped and unexplored interests that aren't part of your current social circle.

2. IN PERSON OR ONLINE, LOCAL OR COMMUTING?

How far are you willing to travel? Do you want to start out virtual and then roll into something in person, or are you ready to jump in?

3. TO JOIN OR CREATE?

Is there a gathering of people that already exists around your Core Interests or is this something you're going to have to start up on your own?

Some Tips

▶ **Community looks different to each of us.** Some people find it easier to connect online; others need faces to look at and group activities to tag along on. Find what feels right for you.

▶ **Don't feel like you have to have something to contribute.** It is okay (at the start) to join a book club or go to the local gathering of hobby wielders and just observe. As you get comfortable, you can jump in with a question or contribution, but for now the main idea is to get yourself out there among others who share the same interests.

Thoughts

▶ Everyone needs a community. Simply put, it reminds us we're not alone, and sometimes that's all the motivation we need to pursue our goal.

▶ It can be hard to really gauge your strengths and weaknesses without interaction with and feedback from others. The people you meet in a community can act as a mirror, reflecting both the good and the "may need some work."

▶ Everyone is a teacher, and that includes you! Communities build reciprocal relationships, so soak up all you can while also imparting your ideas to others.

▶ You don't need to be an expert to join a community or start a group. Exploring for the sake of exploration is enough of a motivator.

Once You're In, Find a Niche Mentor

If you really want to go the extra mile, turn your involvement in your new community into a quest to find a mentor—your Mr. Miyagi (if you've drawn a blank, just do a search for "Karate Kid"). Once you've identified someone, ask her/him to be your mentor. Have a heartfelt message in mind and describe what you seek to learn from them. Look for a way to create repetition in your mentorship: low touch might be just asking them to respond to an emailed question once a month; high touch could be having a conversation over a meal each month. Find something that works for you and your mentor, then put it into practice.

Reflection

1. *Once you got among people who shared the same Core Interest, did you find yourself more excited about that Core Interest?*

2. *What have you learned about the communities that exist around your Core Interest?*

3. *What do you want to investigate deeper?*

"People might have nice ideas: you should be a lawyer, you should be a doctor. Being a lawyer or a doctor is an idea. Every day getting up and having to do what it actually means to be a lawyer or a doctor or a Zen teacher or a carpenter, or whatever you choose—that's the reality of your situation. Life isn't an image. It's actually the doing of it."

—ZEN MASTER BON SOENG, *guiding teacher, Empty Gate Zen Center*

PROJECT #6: TALK WITH SOMEONE WHO'S LIVING YOUR ROADMAP

We've found that there are always people all around us who are doing some aspect of what we dream of doing. And if you can get them on the phone, they're more than willing to talk about how they got to where they are. You just have to ask the questions (in a respectful and courteous manner, of course).

TIME COMMITMENT: High

COSTS: $0–$

SET-UP TIME: About one hour of prep and one hour of conversation

TOOLS/SUPPLIES: Pen and paper, a phone, a willingness to open up and listen

GOAL: To speak with someone who's making a living doing the thing you're interested in

BIG IDEA: Roadtrip Nation started with a pretty simple thought: If you don't know what you want to do in life, find someone who's doing what you're interested in and ask them how they got there. Talking with people is how we've been able to collect all of the insights in this book, and now it's your turn to find your own insights. Get out there and meet real people who are getting paid to do what they love, and ask them how they did it.

Levels of Engagement

LOW: Talk with a friend.

MEDIUM: Reach out to a friend of a friend.

HIGH: Contact someone you're inspired by but have no prior connection to.

RELATED CHAPTERS: *2, 3, 4, 6, 8, 9, 10, 11, 12, 14, 21*

First, Some FAQs

▶ **Why should I do it?**

No profile in a book, no story your friend told you, no idea will ever stand in as a surrogate for real, firsthand experience. The conversations you have will be acts of discovery, revealing the challenges and the excitement that await you on your Roadmap.

▶ **What will I get out of it?**

This is your chance to confirm or reject the ideas you've been chewing on. There's priceless value in getting advice and insights from someone who is living a life in line with your own vision for yourself.

▶ **Isn't this the same as networking?**

No! Networking conversations are the career equivalent of speed dating—each party is on their best behavior, hiding the flawed truths behind a perfectly packaged mask of corporate politeness. The goal of networking isn't to have a deep and meaningful conversation about the tribulations of life; it's to further your own personal occupational agenda. And while that's certainly useful once you've narrowed down your interests, when you're trying to figure out how to build a fulfilling Worklife, you have to go deeper and get personal—you have to talk about LIFE in all of its glories and pitfalls. That's what a Roadtrip Nation conversation is all about.

▶ **Then what is this?**

Forget informational interviewing. This is about developing a conversation with someone who is living out your Roadmap. You'll probably be curious to hear practical details of how this person got to where they are (for example, "Did you have to take organic chemistry for your profession?"), but equally if not more valuable is hearing about their doubts, stumbles, missteps, and other challenges along the road. Get to their personal journey: What were their challenges, and how did they overcome them? When you dispense with the corporate niceties and get real, that person will no longer be just a business card, a job title, or salary; they'll be a complicated human with failures and successes you can learn from.

346

Getting Started

Here are a few things to keep in mind to get you going in the right direction:

▶ **Whom should I talk with?**

Someone who embodies and lives out the things you are interested in. Probably most important, someone who loves what they do. There are plenty of doctors, but you want a doctor who is inspired every day, not someone who's counting the days till retirement. You're looking for insights and stories from someone who is living their own Open Road. Take some time online and do research. List five people who are within reach (geographically speaking).

1.

2.

3.

4.

5.

▶ **What questions should I ask?**

Nothing you can already find online. You want to respect the face-to-face time you have with this person, so don't waste it on things that you could just as easily search. Stay away from company-related questions (like what makes your company's widgets better than the competition's). Sometimes the person's PR autopilot will kick in and they'll feel compelled to speak at length about their company instead of discussing their life journey, so if you sense that happening, try to steer the conversation back toward the personal side of things. This should be a conversation about unpacking the struggles and triumphs of this person's road, so dig beneath the surface and mine their personal story with questions like:

Where were you when you were my age?

Were you ever lost?

What Noise did you hear from others?

Did you ever second-guess yourself?

Did you ever fail?

How did you know the path you were on was the right one?

▶ How do I get people's contact information?

This is where you'll have to be creative. You'll be surprised what you can find online. When given the choice, start with the phone—it's the hardest to do but also the hardest to say no to. If they work at a company, calling the main office number will usually get you somewhere—most often to a personal assistant. Be bold and just ask. Try to avoid the PR departments. Look up people on social media such as Twitter and LinkedIn, where your request would be within a reasonable context.

▶ What if they don't call me back?

Most likely they won't. You'll have to find that balance between persistence and annoyance. When we booked the director of *Saturday Night Live*, one of the original Roadtrippers, Mike, called every few days for three months until Beth answered her phone (while on stage preparing to direct the MTV Music Video Awards). On average, it took making contact with eight people to get one to say yes. If you have any talent for this process (we barely did), your ratio of success should be better than ours, but not by much. That's why we suggested listing five people: it might take that many to get one yes.

348

DOING

Roadtrip Nation began as a complicated excuse for us to talk with really interesting people. We pass on that excuse to you. Use our name as your way in. When you make your first cold call or write that cold email, feel free to say something like this:

"Hi! My name is _____, and I'm interviewing inspiring individuals to learn how they got to where they are today in the hope that it will help me on my own road in life. I would love to talk with you about how you got to where you are today."

Keep in mind that although talking to a stranger may seem intimidating, we've found that once we've done the hard work and gotten through the door, after explaining what we are doing (often to lots of people up the corporate hierarchy), people are more willing to open up and share their stories than you think. In fact, the people we speak with often thank us for the chance to pass on what they've learned.

As you prepare for your conversation, here are the five most important things we've learned for focusing a conversation on someone's road:

▶ **Be yourself.** Often smart people ask the dumbest questions because they are trying to seem even smarter. Typically the younger the person the better the questions tend to be because they are personal and simple. Don't try to seem smart; just be yourself. People are really good at picking up on it when you're not being genuine. Realize that you set the stage. If you're honest and open, the person you're speaking with will be the same.

▶ **Make it personal.** Don't be afraid to be vulnerable. If you'd like someone to open up to you and give you the honest and personal details of their life, you have to open the door first. By sharing information about yourself and being honest about whatever you're struggling with or personal experiences

349

you've had, you will set the tone of the conversation. Also, if you don't give them the personal context for why you'd like to talk to them and what you're looking for, their advice can (and probably will) be way off topic and too general to matter.

▶ **Listen.** The most interesting things will happen when you keep your ears open and chase leads that speak to you as they come up. Try not to think about your next question all the time.

▶ **Go-to questions.** You do not want to spend the whole conversation having to think about your next question. So it's good to have some questions in mind beforehand that can bail you out when you go blank. Keep a few of these in your back pocket to avoid awkward moments.

▶ **Be excited.** Stay engaged. Inside and out. Don't underestimate how far good eye contact, a well-timed "that's interesting" nod, and a firm handshake can take you. We've been on both sides of these. A conversation is what you bring to it. Just like a seesaw—if both parties are pushing off the ground in turn, it gets going fast, but if you come in as dead weight, the conversation isn't going anywhere.

PROJECT #7:
[Invent Your Own Project]

TIME COMMITMENT:

COSTS:

SET-UP TIME:

TOOLS/SUPPLIES:

GOAL:

BIG IDEA:

Levels of Engagement

LOW:

MEDIUM:

HIGH:

Some questions to get started:

1. WHAT AM I DOING?

2. WHY AM I DOING THIS?

3. HOW DOES THIS GET ME CLOSER TO MY OPEN ROAD?

4. HOW AM I PUSHING MY COMFORT ZONE?

5. WHERE DO I START?

▶ **First . . .**

I'll accomplish this by _____.

▶ **Second . . .**

I'll accomplish this by _____.

▶ **Third . . .**

I'll accomplish this by _____.

▶ **Fourth . . .**

I'll accomplish this by _____.

Measure Success

How will I measure my success in this project?

Inspiration

Things related to this project that inspire me:

Reflection

ACKNOWLEDGMENTS

Movies credit the dozens, sometimes hundreds, of people who create them, so why is it that books appear to be made by just a few folks? A book typically lists an author or two, makes some mention (maybe) of an editor and the designer who created the cover, but in movies even the guy who drives the car of the actor's lawyer gets a credit.

The truth is, like just about anything in this world, it takes a village—or in this case, multiple organizations—to make a book. From video editors who turn interview footage into story arcs that move us, to our outreach team who makes cold calls to assistants' interns, to our web team who somehow transforms symbols into clickable magic, everyone here at Roadtrip Nation and at Chronicle Books had a hand (or two) in creating this book you hold in your hands, and they all deserve recognition. So here is the extended movie-style version of the credits for this book:

ROADTRIP NATION

Aaron Farley, *tour coordinator*

Alex Gomez, *director of educational media*

Alyssa Frank, *managing editor/copywriter*

Angie Stalker, *graphic designer*

Annie Mais, *director of education*

Antoine Sanchez, *producer*

Beach Pace, *national sales director*

Brian McAllister, *cofounder*

Cameron Partridge, *senior social media strategist*

Cassie Ehrenberg, *web project manager*

Chelsea Walsh, *pre-editor*

Claire Hauso, *partner relations coordinator*

Craig Polesovsky, *assistant editor*

Dan Ford, *producer*

Elliott Shevchenko, *assistant editor*

Hannah Frankel, *social media coordinator*

Holly Roberts-Dunn, *corporate controller*

Jamie Zehler, *editor*

Jason Manion, *event architect*

Jesse Boels, *assistant editor*

Jordan Myers, *product manager*

Katrina Waidelich, *curriculum writer*

Kelsey Cox, *strategic partnerships manager*

Kevin Strickland, *assistant editor*

Kevin Yamada, *front-end web developer*

Kristen Vedder, *education program logistics*

Lauren Ho, *education program coordinator*

Loureen Ayyoub, *public relations coordinator*

Mara Zehler, *copywriter*

Mark Batstone, *music supervisor and editor*

Melissa Wagasky, *product director*

Mike Marriner, *cofounder*

Molly Gazin, *education program coordinator*

Molly Stelovich, *office manager and accounts payable*

Monique Adcock, *design manager*

Nathan Gebhard, *cofounder, creative director*

Nathan Staph, *assistant editor*

Ryan Lee, *graphic designer*

Scott Conway, *PHP developer*

Tiffany Chow, *partnership strategist*

Willie Witte, *director, professional Roadtripper*

CHRONICLE BOOKS

Albee Dalbotten, *associate marketing director*

Christine Carswell, *publisher*

Jennifer Tolo Pierce, *design director and designer*

Lorena Jones, *publishing director and editor*

Sara Golski, *managing editor*

Stephanie Wong, *marketing and publicity manager*

Steve Kim, *production manager*

THANKS ALSO TO:

Bobby Lee, Brittany Salmon, Caitlin Hawekotte, Chrystal McCluney, Hannah Johnson, James Colannino, Kevin Schaeper, Mariana Iglesias, Ray Ricafort, Sam Wada, Susan Collins, and Tawny Rose.

INDEX

361

362

363

364

NOTES